Mia

A Mother's Story of Loss and Hope

MARISKA ROBBERTS

As told to Colette du Plessis

Published by Crystal Lake Publishing
Website: www.crystallakepub.com

WELCOME
TO ANOTHER

CRYSTAL LAKE PUBLISHING
CREATION

Join today at www.crystallakepub.com & www.patreon.com/CLP

Contents

Preface

We all have a story. The characters differ, the environment is dissimilar, but ultimately there is drama, humour, brokenness and hope in everyone's story. In His mysterious ways, God the eternal Writer weaves our stories together into His own story. Our lives represent an extraordinary paragraph of the all-mighty and all-powerful God's writing that sings his glory.

I have the privilege of being a part of Mariska's story. When you co-write someone's life story, you share in times of happiness and joy, but also in times of trauma and misfortune. In the end, you also share in the hope of good things to come.

Hope and faith are two words that stand out in this story—and in this family's life. It was part of Mia's purpose on earth: to bring hope to the people whose lives she touched.

Is it easy to find hope in hopeless situations? Not at all. But God is faithful, and He has already sown the seeds of hope in the most unlikely places; at the right time they will bear an abundant harvest.

This book is part of the harvest of hope that Mariska found in God's hands. It is an incredible story, with incredible emotions and incredible people...and certainly the (in)credible God.

I am delighted that this story has been written down and published. You and I can find hope in the pages of this book.

All the best with your own story. Know, always, that God is co-writing it with you.

Erika van der Merwe
January 2019
Colorado Springs, USA

hope *noun*

1. a feeling of expectation and desire for a particular thing to happen.

2. a feeling of trust

- definitions from Oxford Languages

The Play of Light

It was nearly April, officially autumn, but in the Boland it still felt like summer.

Vineyards and orchards blurred past as the five members of the Robberts family and Pauline Nugget set out from a guest farm in Klapmuts. People and tractors were hard at work on the farms they passed. But the Robberts family had taken a break from work. It was day three of their holiday, and they had two fun things planned for the day: a pottery workshop on a farm and a lunch date in Stellenbosch.

On Delvera farm, the potter's wheel went round and round as Mom Mariska threw a small pot; Dad Franché also tried his hand at shaping a pot out of clay; Stéfan and Morné painted pots; and little Mia made a mask. The works of clay art were by no means perfect, but the goal of the outing was achieved: the five Robberts family members spent time together. And they played and laughed together.

Excitement about the morning lingered in the air in the Mercedes Vito on their way back to the guest farm, only 10km from Delvera. Just for this one trip, Mia was allowed to sit in front on her mother's lap. Usually she was in the back seat, properly buckled up.

Like an autumn leaf, that's how light she was. Later, she would flutter lightly in the wind on her way to a new destination.

When the red tractor and the grey Vito collided, the occupants couldn't see the play of light.

"I think Miemie is gone," Franché said.

The play of light had begun. But, for now, only the great Potter knew that.

Colette du Plessis

April 2018

5

We humans can distinguish a huge array of colours. Scientists are not entirely certain why, since the ability to see that many colours are not critical for survival. Perhaps we should regard this ability as a gift, a token of love from the Creator, encouraging us to enjoy life.

Blue I

Blue is the colour of the heavens.

In the beginning

She was home for a week before she had to go back to the hospital. She had developed mild pneumonia, probably due to an excess of kisses from her two older brothers. Still, 2009 was a good year. Mia Ananja Robberts was the first of the Robberts siblings not to be rushed to the neonatal unit immediately after birth. Like other healthy babies, she could share a hospital room with her mother, and then go home with her mother.

Mia did have to have surgery for an intestinal obstruction in the first few weeks of her life. At the time she held a record at a well-known Bloemfontein hospital for the youngest baby ever who'd had an appendix removed.

Barely a month old and already a record breaker. Inside me, however, something else broke that day.

The wait outside the operating theatre doors felt like an eternity. In the first 24 hours I wasn't allowed to pick her up. She cried bitterly. The doctors didn't want to give her too much pain medication, partly because she was so little. Meanwhile, my breasts felt like bursting from all the milk and my baby's crying.

After the operation it looked as if her tummy had been stitched up using a sewing machine. She had a distinct zigzag pattern almost 5 cm long across her abdomen. Weeks later it still looked like the incision had not healed completely; there was a hole in which my finger could fit.

We went back to the paediatrician, and he determined that she had developed a hernia. She had to have another operation. But I told him I was going to pray for the hole to close up on its own. He laughed and said we should go on holiday first and then make another appointment to see him.

I resolved not to let Mia go under the knife again. In the days following the diagnosis of a hernia I kept praying for a miracle. I was convinced the hole was getting smaller. After the holiday, spent swimming in the sea and praying, we went back to the doctor. The surgeon confirmed there was a hole, but she wanted to wait before operating again. Within a few weeks the hole had disappeared completely.

The joy of having a healthy baby girl finally became a reality.

It was a completely different experience from bringing up my two sons. Not better, just different. Like playing with a doll, I dressed her in pretty clothes. I bathed her, put lotion on her skin, changed her nappies and fed her. I was a girl mom, and we were all truly happy.

The years went by. As Mia grew older, we got to know her as anything but a quiet, reserved little girl. She was exuberant. She laughed with her mouth open. She could get furious. She did everything to excess. And we loved her excessively.

It's only a wee-wee
In the last few weeks of the first school term of 2013, Mia was irritable and tearful. She was also more clingy than usual; she wouldn't let me out of her sight.

I knew she was tired and that the long, busy term had taken its toll. Mia just needed a little extra love, but it was difficult to find the time in between her brothers' activities and my work commitments. I would sometimes put her in the car and go for a drive, and she would sleep for the entire trip. But every time we had to get out of the car, she would

cry. There wasn't much more I could do. Alone time with her simply had to wait for our forthcoming holiday in the Cape.

As usual before going on holiday, the day before our departure I had numerous tasks to tick off my to-do list. I was frustrated by all the things I couldn't seem to get done, and with my frustration came impatience. With Mia too. She didn't even want to go to the bathroom on her own to have a wee. My irritation at her brief helplessness that day would haunt me for years.

On holiday!

We left Bloemfontein on Friday, 22 March 2013, towing a full trailer. Our main destination was Stellenbosch. As usual on a long car journey the children repeatedly asked how far we had left to go. Mia was part of the choir. She wanted to know how far it still was to "Skelmbos," her name for the town where– as the word "*skelm*" (villain) foreshadows—she would be stolen from us.

We stayed over for one night on a farm near Three Sisters in the Karoo. Next to the farm road there were two crosses. Only later that evening would I find out about the freak accident that had happened on that farm: a father accidentally drove over both his children. It struck a deep chord of empathy in my heart. Travelling with children in the car, we couldn't help but be deeply affected by this family's pain.

I woke up the next morning to silence except for the sound of leaves rustling in the wind. This was in stark contrast to the hurry-scurry of the previous few weeks. After breakfast we walked to a Bloekombos tree[1] next to the farmhouse and took our first family photos of the holiday, as always gathering new memories of special moments. That's after all what holidays are for!

It was late afternoon when we arrived at our cottage on the guest farm not far from Stellenbosch that would be our home for the holiday, a lovely place with a stunning view over the vineyards. It was exactly what we'd hoped for.

---

1. Eucalyptus globulus, commonly known as southern blue gum or blue gum.

Over the next few days we criss-crossed the Cape Peninsula, but in the evenings we were back at our farm cottage. From our porch the sunsets were even more spectacular than from Camps Bay Beach. That's what we thought anyway. There was one evening at sunset in particular when God reminded us that He was close by.

On the morning of Tuesday, 26 March, Dad and the boys went golfing, and Mia and I stayed home. With nothing planned, I had plenty of time to play along when Mia asked me to make up her face too. This was the day I was going to give her the full treatment, I decided: foundation, eye shadow, even mascara. She could indulge in what would be a no-no on any other day.

I also blow-dried her hair until there was not a single girly curl left. She looked breath-takingly beautiful.

When she saw herself in the mirror, she was also struck speechless. Then she ran to the kitchen to show Pauline what she looked like.

I never captured that moment on camera.

Mia couldn't wait for her Daddy to get back. When she heard the car driving up and stopping outside, she hid from him. Then, as quietly as a three-year-old in "play" high heels could tiptoe, she sneaked up on him. She waited for the right moment to startle him with a deafening *"Wha!"* The usual "Whose princess are you?" game followed. Franché tickled her until she acknowledged she was her Daddy's princess, and only his.

Mostly, Mia laughed (exuberantly) 90% of the time and experienced (overwhelming) anger 10% of the time. During this holiday the anger was absent.

That evening the sunset was the pinkest of pinks. There was an almost-full moon, which lightened the night sky.

The holiday was exactly what I'd been looking forward to.

Black

Black is the total absence of light or colour.

Wednesday, 27 March 2013

We rose early and got ready for our special family morning on the farm Delvera. We wanted to try our hand at pottery. Just after our arrival I knocked my camera's LCD screen against something and it broke. It was a disappointment, but I was happy to discover that I could still take photos by looking through the optical viewfinder.

We painted small clay pots, made masks out of clay and even tried to throw pots on the pottery wheel. I took lots of photographs.

Everyone was in such high spirits. When we left at 10 o'clock, Mia skipped rather than walked to the car.

Our next stop was KFC. There was much merriment in the Vito minivan as each child tried to outshout the others to order their favourite KFC meal. Amid the excitement about pops, chips and mash, Franché missed the turn-off we should have taken. Once we'd found Bottelary Road, our plans for the day were back on track.

I've always been the seatbelt enforcer in the family. On school days I ask the children what seems like a hundred times to fasten their seatbelts. During the school terms I have to keep to a strict schedule to fit in everything and everyone. There's no time for dawdling, which is why I sometimes lose my temper over the seatbelt issue. That day I didn't. We were on holiday. And I cherish holidays for the time we as a family can spend together just being happy and relaxed.

That morning, I didn't say, "Buckle up." Why? Maybe I had relaxed too much, so much so that I had already forgotten the normal rhythm and routine of our life at home. Little did I know what it would cost me.

As Franché pulled out to overtake a car, he saw a tractor ahead of it trundling along, straddling the lane line. He decided to accelerate and pass the tractor too—oncoming cars were far enough away to pass it safely.

As we drew level with the tractor, the driver suddenly turned right. "Franché, watch out!" I shouted. He swung the steering wheel to the right to avoid colliding with the tractor...but it was too late.

There was a loud bang. We'd hit the tractor. In the next few seconds, it felt as if we were gliding through the air. There was, I think, a moment of silence. That's all I can remember of the accident.

Later, I heard our Vito minivan had hit the roadside barrier and rolled three times, down an embankment. When it came to a standstill, Franché jumped out immediately; I struggled a little to get out.

We heard both boys crying.

I saw Pauline and Morné sitting on the grass, slightly apart. Pauline sat with her legs straight out in front of her, her headscarf askew. Morné had an enormous lump on the side of his face; he was covered in blood.

Stéfan was still in the minivan. I pulled him out through a window and put him down on the grass next to Pauline. Then I dragged Morné closer to them. Stéfan's nose was bleeding heavily. I tried to console and calm them. They wanted to know where Mia was.

That's when I ran to the other side of the minivan and saw Franché sitting next to Mia. She was lying there, not moving at all. I was convinced she was just unconscious and went back to the boys. But after a while I returned to where Franché was sitting with Mia.

"I think Miemie is gone," he said.

I refused to believe it.

A story I'd once read leapt to my mind. Public speaker Retha McPherson related the story of a man who'd stopped at the scene of an accident and called out, "In the mighty name of Jesus Christ, this boy will live! He will not die!" I started to pray out loud, in tongues, as I ran back and forth between Pauline and the boys and Franché and Mia. I did it over and over. Back and forth. Again and again.

Then I got into the minivan to gather our shoes, CDs and other personal belongings, because it had suddenly occurred to me that people's things were often stolen at the scene of an accident. A few farm workers approached us; one of them gave me a white hessian bag in which I could place our things.

It was as if time had stopped.

At one point I stood still next to Franché and Mia and I looked at her for a moment. Her little face looked perfect and calm. But her skin was so pale. Too pale.

The day was black.

There wasn't a drop of blood visible on Mia's body or face. Her dress had shifted up a bit and I saw that her tummy with the zigzag scar was flat; she didn't have her little pot belly anymore.

In the meantime, a number of people had stopped to offer help. I phoned the emergency number of Mediclinic Bloemfontein, simply because I had the number saved on my phone for those nights when one of the children would suddenly get a high fever and we'd need to get them to the hospital quickly. When the woman on the other end of the line asked me where we were, I couldn't tell her. I ran up the embankment and handed my phone to a stranger so he could describe our location. I knew there was a Mediclinic private hospital in Stellenbosch; we'd driven past it before. And I trusted they would get someone to come and help us.

When I got back to Franché and Mia, I took a good look at her. I noticed that her neck was lying at an unnatural angle. At the back of her head I saw blood. It also looked as if a part of the back of her head was gone. I looked at the grass around me and saw a greyish jelly-like substance that brought to mind a drawing in a school biology handbook from long ago.

I recognised it as brain tissue. This was later confirmed: Mia's brain injury was fatal. That's when it first sunk in that she could really be gone.

Still I ran between my children, around the wreck that lay between them. The boys kept asking, "Where is Mia?" I told them she was unconscious, but when my eyes met Pauline's I silently shook my head. She whispered something in Sotho[1]. She kept comforting the boys, keeping them calm. She was a rock that day. She had been my right hand for nearly 15 years.

In the meantime Franché and I had started to ask people if there was anyone with medical training. A man took Mia's pulse, and he confirmed that she was dead.

My husband started to wail; grief escaped in guttural cries from deep inside him.

I felt detached.

The boys, who must have realised then that their little sister had died, also started to cry. It only occurred to me later that up to that moment they had had no concept of death.

The ambulance arrived soon thereafter. I was with the boys and Pauline while the paramedics assessed them.

At one stage I walked back to Mia, who was now covered with a white cloth. I lifted it, kissed her and said goodbye. A paramedic put her arm around me when I got up to go back to my boys.

The wind had come up and the ambulance driver had put my handbag on the corner of the cloth so it wouldn't blow off my little princess.

---

1. Sesotho, also known as Southern Sotho, is an indigenous African Language.

On the other side of the Vito, Morné cried when a paramedic touched his arm. "I don't want to die! I don't want to die!" he shrieked. Around Stéfan's nose the blood had dried to a dark crust.

Then our family got into the ambulance, without Mia. The boys couldn't understand why we were leaving her there. I felt a crushing burden of despair having to leave my child there in the field next to the road in a strange place, being driven away from her.

Only once we were in the ambulance did I feel my hip and shoulder start to throb with pain. A man asked me questions in order to fill in a form. A siren sounded from time to time. A very kind woman dressed in green told the boys where we were going and why they were using the siren.

I phoned Thea, with whom we were supposed to have lunch in Stellenbosch. And I phoned my sister and my aunt in Pretoria and asked them to tell my mother and father what had happened.

When we arrived at the hospital, Thea was already there. It was good to see a familiar face. Heinrich and Hannelie, friends from Durbanville, were also there. I would later learn that Heinrich had been at the scene of the accident. Certain things that happened next to Bottelary Road got seared into my brain; others, such as the fact that Heinrich had been there, were wiped from my memory.

Franché, Stéfan, Morné and I were together in a hospital room. We'd requested that Pauline also be treated at Mediclinic and not at a state hospital. The tractor driver was in the room next to ours.

Lying on the hospital bed, Stéfan looked at me and said, rolling his r's, "Mommy, you were right. You always say we should fasten our seatbelts, and just look what happened." His words cut through me like a keen-edged knife.

Doctors and nurses started to clean off the blood from my sons with white cloths. The four of us were overwhelmed with grief and shock.

I only started to cry when I phoned the friends we'd stayed over with in the Karoo a few days previously to tell them what had happened. A nurse gave me a pill to put under my tongue. There was a narrow corridor leading to an X-ray room... I don't remember anything else.

Much later, Heinrich and Hannelie took us home in a rented minivan. "Home" was the lovely farm cottage. I lay down on my bed. When I think back now, not much comes to mind. There's really very little I can remember about the rest of the day. I heard later that Hannelie spent the whole evening there and looked after everyone. Franché's sister, Ilzette, and her husband, Richard, were there too, someone told me later. They wanted to take us to their house in Somerset West, but I refused to go.

Neville Goodchild, our pastor and good friend from Bloemfontein, flew to Cape Town within hours of hearing the news and somehow made it to our cottage. His gentle voice was a comfort as we talked and prayed. He slept on an uncomfortable bench in our cottage, which now seemed empty and cold.

In the morning he responded to a question of mine from the previous evening: "Neville, will I see her again?" He opened his Bible and read Isaiah 49:15–23 to me:

15 [The Lord answered] "Can a woman forget her nursing child
    And have no compassion on the son of her womb?
    Even these may forget, but I will not forget you.
    16 "Indeed, I have inscribed [a picture of] you on the palms *of My hands*;
    Your city walls [Zion] are continually before Me.
    17 "Your builders hurry;
    Your destroyers and devastators
    Will go away from you.

[18] "Lift up your eyes and look around [at the returning exiles];

All these gather together and they come to you [to rebuild you].

As I live," declares the Lord,

"You [Zion] will indeed clothe yourself with all of them as jewels
and tie them on as a bride.

[19] "For your ruins and desolate places and your land [once the
scene] of destruction—

Certainly now [in the coming years] will be too cramped for the
inhabitants,

And those who *once* engulfed you will be far away.

[20] "The children of your bereavement [those born in captivity] will
yet say in your ears,

'The place is too cramped for me';

Make room for me that I may live *here*.

[21] "Then [Zion], you will say in your heart,

'Who has borne me these *children*,

Since I have been bereaved of my children

And am barren, an exile and a wanderer?

And who has reared these?

Indeed, I was left alone;

From where then did these *children* come?'"

[22] This is what the Lord God says:

"Listen carefully; I will lift up My hand to the [Gentile]nations

And set up My banner to the peoples;

And they will bring your sons in the fold of their garments,

And your daughters will be carried on their shoulders.

[23] "Kings will be your attendants,

And their princesses your nurses.

They will bow down to you with their faces to the earth

And lick the dust of your feet;

And you shall know [with an understanding based on personal experience] that I am the Lord;

For they shall not be put to shame who wait *and* hope expectantly for Me.

Hope... Perhaps.

Thursday, 28 March 2013

While Franché and I waited at the police station to formally identify Mia's body, I got a message on my phone. Someone had sent me a link to an article in *Volksblad* newspaper about our accident. I read it, as well as the comments below the article. Someone upbraided me for not ensuring the children were buckled up. The mother of a learner who went to the same school as my sons had responded to that comment with, "Never pass on a good opportunity to shut up."

In the meantime, I was waiting to identify the body of my child. And I knew: I'd already imprisoned myself. Me, the mother who sometimes would brake abruptly if the children hadn't yet fastened their seatbelts to impress on them the seriousness of the situation. Me, the mother who really tried to teach my children the habit of always wearing their seatbelts. Me, the mother who now had to stand in front of a glass window looking into a narrow room.

I could only see her face, not the rest of her body, as she was swathed in white cloths. White as snow. Unblemished, except for a very small mark on her eyelid that looked like a dried tear.

I now knew the origin of the expression "as pale as death".

Between me and her there was a glass window. It was difficult not to think of the fact that I would never again be able to touch her soft, plump body.

The one dark thought followed the other.

Never again would I hear her laugh.

Never again would she skip towards me.

Never again would I comb tangles out of her hair. Never again would I paint her nails.

Never again.

At the funeral parlour in Strand an assistant wanted to know how tall Mia was—how many centimetres? I didn't know. It had never mattered. But now it mattered: Mia had to fit in a coffin.

Next to the busy road where my life had been torn apart, we as a family stood once again to plant a small white cross with a pink ribbon tied around it. Some of us still had scabs, some had bruises, but every one of us had a broken heart.

Not far from there was a signpost showing the way to the farm "Swartrivier, Stellenrust," a name that translates as Black River, which now took on a grim significance.

I sat down on the grass next to the road. The posts that had formed the road safety barrier were broken. As was I.

Franché walked down the embankment to where she had lain. Someone had poured sand on the spot, and among the small piles of sand he picked up pink and purple beads from a strand she'd worn. Jewels of plastic, he'd call them later.

We got back into the minivan. I tried to explain to my sons that the ragdoll body of their little sister was no longer important. It was her spirit, which was now with Jesus, that mattered. It's hard to explain such things to young children.

Back at the cottage on the farm, we started to pack. Mia's headbands, blonde hairs still clinging to some of them; the drawings she'd made the previous day; her yellow princess pyjamas that she'd taken off that morning...I stuffed everything of hers into my bag.

We left the idyllic farm cottage like exiles; a dream holiday was in ruins.

We settled in at Ilzette and Richard's house in Somerset West, armed with medication for the pain. It felt as if everything around me was hazy. I've since heard it referred to as heavenly anaesthesia; they say it calms your mind so you can move dispassionately from one crying jag to the next. Little did I know that those first waves of tears would be low tide still.

Franché and I went for a walk that afternoon to escape from the house. Along the way we sat down on a fallen tree trunk and we talked: I said that I forgave him, and he said that he forgave me. On that lifeless log we made a pact never to blame each other for Mia's death.

Looking back, I know it's one of the best things we could have done. In the months that followed we had to remind each other of that pact numerous times.

A letter to myself

On Thursday, 28 March 2013, like I've been doing on most days of my adult life, I wrote in my diary. In many ways, this habit saved me from derangement. When it felt to me as if everything inside me was threatening to tear skin and break bone, I wrote...like this letter to myself that I wrote the day after Mia's death:

My life changed irrevocably on 27 March 2013 at 10:50 on Bottelary Road at Swartrivier farm, Stellenrust, Stellenbosch.

Our Miemie Muis[2] was stolen from us by "Skelmbos". But Jesus took her back and said: "Satan, she is Mine."

The rest of us, Franché, Stéfan, Morné, Pauline and I, walked away with just a few scratches.

How do you begin to understand it?

Guilt creeps in like cockroaches creeping from crevices.

But amid the unbearable, unreal hurt, I know God is in control.

My Miemie Muis, my Nonna[3], my Princess is lying in God's arms tonight.

It's terribly hard for me to know I won't see her again for a very long time. I am torn between two worlds, because I want to stay here on earth for my husband and my sons, but my heart is drawn to heaven because I want so much to be with Mia. I'll miss out on so much until I see her again.

---

2. How Mia pronounced Minnie Mouse.

3. Another word for small little lady of the house.

Won't she come out of the room now with sleep-tangled hair? My dearest, dearest little angel. Mommy misses you more than words can say. There are things that Mommy still has to do here, which is why Jesus didn't take me too. He still has a few plans for me. But wait in our little cottage, my princess. Mommy will be there in a little while.

Friday, 29 March 2013
On Good Friday we returned to the funeral home in Strand. I was really grateful that they were willing to open up especially for us. There, I put my little Mia, enclosed in a wooden urn with a plaque (featuring a wrong date of death), in my handbag.

That afternoon we set out for Bloemfontein. It was comforting to know she was going home with us.

It's odd how something can suddenly become vital, I thought at one point. Having an urn filled with her ashes in my handbag seemed to me a singular necessity.

Grey

Grey is without emotion and pointless. It has no connection with any-thing or anyone. Grey does not belong.

Flowers at the gate

When we arrived at our house in Bloemfontein, there were three bunches of flowers on the grass in front of our gate, each placed in a water-filled bag. It was the first time I'd seen this inventive way of delivering flowers when no one's at home to receive them.

An empty house, an empty bed, empty arms.

I remember that first weekend back home as a time when people came and went—as if it were a train station, me sitting on a bench as people walked up and down past me. Some brought things; others came to sit with us, quietly or uncomfortably; still others talked about anything but death.

Bunches and bunches of flowers were delivered to our door, until the florist eventually called to say she was holding some orders back until the first flowers had started to wilt. People dropped off numerous dishes of food, lasagne being a popular choice. I pecked at food reluctantly; I felt as if I would choke on it.

Our two dachshunds, Mia's woo-woos, didn't want to get off my lap during those first few days we were back home—and when I did get up they would follow me everywhere. Named Lientjie and Dantjies, they were gifts to Mia on her second birthday.

In a daze, I somehow got through the first few days. Whenever I saw something Mia had liked, I moved it to the dining table, turning it into a shrine of sorts. Amid the growing pile of Mia's favourite things we lit a small pink candle, which we kept burning day and night.

Just like I kept carrying Mia's things to the dining table, so people kept bringing us stuff. Dear Pauline again put our family above her own and stayed with us that first weekend to help us tidy up once the visitors had gone. Everyone wanted to help, but nothing helped.

Nothing.

Every breath hurt. I felt exhausted when I went to bed, and I felt exhausted when I got up.

Today, I can only describe it as a kind of numbness.

In the first week of April 2013 I wrote another letter to myself…or rather, to Mia:

Mia, I'm sorry I was so angry and impatient with you that day at Aunt Charlene's when you didn't want to go wee-wee on your own. It was wrong of Mommy. I was rushed and I just wanted to get everything done before we left on holiday.

Thank you for all the times you were a ray of sunshine in Mommy's minivan, cheering us all up.

I loved it when you would jostle you brothers out of the way to lie in my arms, or "ammy," as you called it, and we'd call you our little buffalo.

Lying in on a Saturday morning was precious to Mommy, because we're both late risers.

I miss your tangled hair that you didn't want combed out; I even miss your cupboard doors always being left open.

I'm thinking of the day Mommy had to take Stéfan and Mornéto have ID photos taken for the chess league, when you stepped up to pose for a photo too. That photo is still in my wallet.

When you accompanied me to do the shopping at Pick'nPay and finished a punnet of strawberries before we'd got to the till—I miss that too.

Oh, and do you remember the day we were at On Tap, where you can buy everything for the bathroom, when you wanted to wee-wee in a toilet in the showroom?

There are so many memories, Mia. The pink dresses I had to buy at Woolworths, and the pink bolero jacket that you refused to take off, causing quite a to-do in the shop. And I wonder why I'm remembering your ravenous appetite for sweets—I wish I hadn't thrown away any of the poorly concealed sweet wrappers.

I'm writing to you to remember—to remember that *Tangled* was your favourite DVD, and to remember your sneaky naps in the dachshunds' basket.

How will I ever be able to go on with my life without you in it?

A pink service

Organising events is something I'm good at; it was, after all, my profession for many years. But all your work experience counts for nothing when you have to organise your own child's memorial service. I made dozens of calls, got quotations, and then, suddenly, I'd be confronted with the reason for all the arrangements. Deciding which photographs to use in the pamphlet for the church service tore my heart into pieces. Fortunately, close friends and former colleagues made suggestions when I couldn't make a choice.

My eldest sister, whom I hadn't been close to for a number of years, was suddenly by my side.

My mother, in her quiet way, tried to be strong for my sake and to support me in any way she could, even though her heart was also broken over her daughter's anguish and her own sorrow as a grandmother. A mother will always be a mother, no matter how old her daughter is. Her daughter's grief is also her own grief.

It was a pink service, from the flowers and the table linen to the sweets for Mia's playmates. We even asked everyone who attended the service to wear pink.

Just as the colour of the day was Mia's favourite, it was important that the music would also be her choice. Besides "Until I'm Home" by Nianell, which a friend suggested, all the other songs we played at the memorial service were ones to which she and her dad, her fellow music lover, regularly danced. On the playlist for the pink service were "Kaptein" by Kurt Darren (or "Patyn", as Mia called it); "Skarumba" by Juanita du Plessis ("Skumba"); "Boerejol", also by Juanita du Plessis ("Boetie en Sussie");and, for Franché and Mia's final dance, "I'm a Barbie Girl".

Bye-bye, my darling

It was a Saturday afternoon. I chose not to take a sedative before the service. In the church garden, off to one side, out of sight of the people who'd arrived early, I asked God to give me the strength to get through the day. I wanted to speak at the service.

People had come from all over. My brother had travelled from Switzerland; fortunately he could get a connecting flight to Bloemfontein and be in time for the service. I hadn't been aware we knew that many people, let alone that many people with young daughters who'd wear pink tutus.

We had chosen to celebrate Mia's life with this service, because she had been the best example of having life in abundance, as the Bible says in John 10:10. She lived much more in her three-and-a-bit years than many people manage to fit into 20 years. (Weeks after Mia's death, an acquaintance comforted me with these exact words.)

I now remember how I trembled as I was talking about Mia. How I implored people, all with stony faces or tears running down their

cheeks, not to stop praying for us. Franché also spoke that Saturday afternoon. His words were few, but profound.

Is it possible that photos flashed on a screen are all you have left of your child?

Everything on the sweets table had been eaten. The pink guests had left.

A veil of one great, bizarre unreality was drawn over the day. Like fuzzy pink candyfloss.

The new term

When the new school term started on a Tuesday in April, I took the brave step of going to Mia's pre-primary school, Bambi. I took what was left of the large princess cake we'd had at the memorial service for the kids to enjoy.

The bitter firsts without Mia were not limited to the first Christmas or the first birthday or the first seaside holiday or the first whatever—they included the simple acts of walking down the vegetable aisle in Pick'nPay or through the children's clothing section in Woolworths.

And I also cried the second, third and fourth times, just a little less each time.

"The first cut is the deepest." I can attest to that.

Something Bishop T.D. Jakes once said often helped me—I can still hear him saying it in his heavy accent: "Even if I do it afraid, but I will do it." In my version of his words, I've added something: "Even if I do it afraid, with tears running down my face, but I will do it. I will face the giants everywhere I go."

At Bambi Pre-Primary every child wore a pink mourning band around his or her wrist. My visit turned into an event. We planted a pink Candy Stripe rose for Mia. It seemed to me as if I wasn't planting the rose but rather burying it. The smell of damp soil and my heartache became more intense with every scoop of soil that filled the pot.

Later that afternoon I had to fetch my sons at Willem Postma Primary School. One and all who saw me gave me a hug, even people I didn't know. It felt as if it would simply never stop. There were, however, also mothers who took cover behind trees and pointed at me as they talked among themselves (about Mia's death, I assumed). I felt terribly exposed.

It was a very, very difficult and emotionally challenging day. Long and painful. And so were the days, weeks and months that followed. Life gradually returned, like a foot that had fallen asleep that was stinging with pins and needles.

Tuesday, 9 April 2013

So I wrote again, but this time not a letter to myself or to Mia. Late one evening I typed a text message to my aunt, a medical doctor:

Tannie[1], Mia's neck was broken and she died of head injuries. I think it was her brain tissue I saw lying on the grass near her body. Do you think she died instantly when she hit the windscreen? Or could she have felt anything as she was lying there on the grass? When Franché got to her after the car had come to a standstill, it looked to him like she was dead.

Her answer:

No, she would have died instantly and she would not have felt a thing. She would not even have realised what was happening to her.

I wrote back:

So the last thing she was aware of was that she was in my arms? Because it felt to me like it happened so incredibly fast. I didn't feel her slipping out of my arms or had time to think that I had to hold on to her. She just went from my arms into Jesus' arms?

Her answer:

Definitely. She would have woken up in heaven in Jesus' arms. Try to sleep now and in your mind's eye see her in heaven playing with angels. Ask the Lord to show her to you so it can bring you innerpeace.

Diary: Wednesday, 10 April 2013

I wrote in my diary again. Was it a prayer? Or was it a plea?

Dear Lord, allow me to see her and hold her again in my dreams. Show me that she is there with You and that she is happy. I know everyone says she is with You, Lord, but I so desperately want to see it for myself, and thus find miraculous peace. Lord, hold my husband and me tightly in your embrace and help us to grow ever closer to each other. I know it's the enemy's plan to use our deep hurt and confused emotions to come between us, but I will not allow it. I've fought too hard to make our marriage work. Lord, protect our family from more arrows of death that the enemy sends towards us.

Dear Lord, fill this huge hole in my heart with Your peace. Grant me strength so I will stop feeling this paralysed, as if I'm just staggering onwards, carried by built-up momentum. Lord, help me, please!

Lord, I write to You because it is easier than praying. The heartache gets too much when I pray, and the words won't come.

Dear Lord, I still love You, even though you allowed my little girl to die. I am not angry; I just don't understand. It feels a little unfair to me. I thought we had enough challenges in our life. You know about the boys' daily battle with their bodies. I never thought such a terrible thing would cross our path too.

I realise that I won't understand it now, but, Lord, just hold me tightly.

I love You very much.

Diary: Thursday, 11 April 2013

Today was a bad day, having had to reorganise my schedule for the boys' extracurricular activities, planning when I'd be dropping them off and picking them up afterwards. I simply could not bring myself to do it on the computer, like I always did before, because it would have meant seeing the lines for Mia's Kindermusik and Dance Mouse classes and having to delete them. I couldn't face it.

So there I sat with a half-hearted handwritten schedule in front of me. Where was the super-organised Mariska with her Excel spread-sheets?

Diary: Friday, 12 April 2013

I think I am in denial. I cry now and then, but the rest of the time I am in a state of inertia and I don't know what to do with myself in this powerless state. It feels as if Mia has just gone to play with a friend; she'll be back soon.

It's almost like your first day in a new job. You don't really know what to do, whether to stand around and wait for someone to give you an assignment, or make coffee, or do some filing. And you don't know where the bathroom is.

I'm usually the one with the plans and the lists, ready to fix everything. And now, now I'm numb.

Everyone wants to come over for coffee. Friends and strangers. Acquaintances and busybodies. Everyone has offered help: they want to do our shopping, give our children lifts and cook our meals.

I start to sneak in at the school when I drop the boys off. I don't want anyone to notice me. Yet there is always someone around a corner who stops me, and then I cry uncontrollably. I realise people want to help and they care and they mean well. But does it really help? It feels to me as if it just makes everything worse to be confronted with reality again and again.

People who've never, ever before in their lives wanted to have coffee with me, wanted to do so now. After such a coffee date I feel as if I'm only doing it to please them. I know it sounds petty, but it's how I feel.

I am tired of having coffee. People are often unsure about what to say or do. And I'm the most unsure of all. I don't know how to "be" at all.

So, we make small talk.

It feels as if I've been dropped off in the middle of China and I'm expected to carry on with my life on foreign soil.

Pink

The phrase "in the pink" means healthy; the expression "tickled pink"
means being happy, content.
– bournecreative.com

The phrase "to pink" means to create a small cut.
– dictionary.com

Yearning

Franché and I had yearned to have a third child, despite the fact that doctors had diagnosed Stéfan and Morné with a muscle condition that was, medically speaking, incurable. I went for tests to find out whether I carried the gene for the condition. The wait for the results felt like an eternity. During that "eternity" we decided to move forward in faith with another pregnancy. This journey of faith was coloured pink from the outset.

By the time Mia made her appearance, it was neon pink.

I wanted her *so* much. We all did. And then she arrived, like a spring blossom after winter. And she was healthy. The time after her birth was one of the happiest periods of my life.

We lavishly celebrated Mia's life in pink, from the beginning to the end.

Friday, 19 April 2013

I was praying in my room. I prayed in tongues, and then it happened...

I saw my Miemie Muis in a white dress with a bright-pink shoulder sash. Her blonde locks were silky and without tangles; I could almost feel her soft hair between my fingers. She was gazing at me with a contented expression on her face. She had a look of resignation in her eyes, like she'd sometimes given me when I had to go away for work and she had to stay behind with Pauline.

A source of light above her head illuminated her face slightly. Her teeth were a brilliant white. She laughed open-mouthed and started to play on the green lawn of a garden that was so beautiful it took my breath away. There were all kinds of animals, and she was playing with them.

In my vision Mia wore a long, almost too long, white dress; I couldn't see her feet. She somersaulted and rolled on the grass. She looked happy and she was laughing.

I saw Mia asking Jesus to pick her up. There were other people in the garden, too, all dressed in white. Mari, a friend we lost to leukaemia years ago, was among them. With her long, dark hair and olive skin, she stood next to Jesus, her eyes gentle.

Later, Jesus was holding Mia on his hip. Everyone was smiling. I asked Mari to take good care of Mia, and I gave her an instruction: Give her lots of hugs! Mari smiled, nodded and put her arms around Mia while Jesus was still holding her.

The other people, whose faces I couldn't see, waved to me. Mia touched her palms to her lips and blew the kiss towards me, like she always used to do.

Then she began to move her hands faster and faster, sending me a stream of kisses. Jesus handed Mia to Mari.

Everyone was waving to me as the image gradually blurred, like when you zoom out from something you'd focused on with a camera. The group of people turned around and walked towards hills dotted with white houses.

A day later, in my brownish-grey house, I wrote in my diary after I'd read the following passage in my Joyce Meyer Bible:

As you consider how many times you have already come to the other side, of pain, you can be confident, you will make it again through Christ who strengthens you (see Philippians 4:13). And on the other side of trials, you will see how God turned those experiences into good for your life (see Romans 8:28)...

42

When you are tempted to become disconnected, remember, "This too shall pass." Your afflictions are "light and momentary" from the perspective of eternity.

No matter how bad your current situation may look, God loves you! Never let go of the truth that God loves you, no matter what happens in your life. You can trust that everything will work out because of His great love for you.

I am sorry, Lord. This message is not a reality for me yet. And I apologise for the bewilderment and all the questions and my inability to make sense of it.

It is not my intention to trouble you. I battle with my pain and I puzzle over things in my heart. Help me to get through this.

Help my husband and our sons and me to come out on the other side of this trial and to experience You again the way we should. To experience joy, peace, prosperity and favour again. I know it's what you have planned for us—we just have to recognise and accept it. Help me to do that.

Thank You for Your solace and grace. Thank You for showing me Mia yesterday morning.

Pink tulips

So, nearly every day, I sought comfort at the feet of the Lord. Sometimes I only cried, but most of the time I wrote. I wrote what was in my heart because I couldn't get the words out any other way—it simply hurt too much.

On 22 April, three days after the special experience in my room, I was sitting on a bench under a tree at my sons' school, waiting for the bell to ring to signal the end of the school day. I saw her approaching me...a blonde woman I only knew by sight. A beautiful woman. She was a member of our congregation, so I knew that she knew our story. In her hands she had a bunch of bright-pink tulips, a really bright pink.

"I don't know you," she said to me. "But...the Lord has laid it on my heart for a few days now to give you a bouquet of pink flowers with pink angel's hair in it. He showed me what the flowers should look like."

Even the pink angel's hair? I wondered.

And then she said the few sprigs she held between her fingers were the only angel's hair the florist had. If they hadn't been pink, they would have been near invisible. Every now and then the breeze picked up the "hairs" before they settled on her fingers again.

"The Lord wanted me to tell you that the dream you had about your little girl had to be confirmed." Just like that.

And then she spoke a little faster. "May you find strength. We are praying for you."

We don't see many tulips in Bloemfontein, and here in South Africa they usually bloom in winter. They were perfect for this icy season of my life, I thought.

And on that day, 22 April 2013, hope became a part of my life again. I now knew I hadn't thought up the dream about Mia.

This was my diary prayer on that day:

Thank You very much, Heavenly Father, that, even though I sometimes feel as if there were a chasm between Jesus and me, You're actually very close to me and You see and feel my pain.

I want to ask You to show my husband and me more of these images or dreams. Lord, I ask that she may continue to live before my mind's eye so we can hold on to Your promises that we will see her again, with You, one day.

Just then, someone sent me the following SMS:

Can anything separate us from the love of Christ? Can trouble, suffering, and hard times, or hunger and nakedness, or danger and death?
– Romans 8:35 (CEV)

I jotted down the following sentence in my diary after getting the floral gift, after my prayer, and after reading the SMS:

Not even death can separate me from You, Heavenly Father.

26 April 2013

It's difficult to find the words to describe the sunset I saw from my bedroom balcony this evening. There were a few dark clouds and lots of pink, red and orange streaks running through them. It was beautiful. It was dramatic. It looked a little like molten lava forcing its way through the dark clouds—a lethal lava flow incinerating everything in its path. Maybe a symbol of the suffocating pain I was feeling inside of me? Just left of the setting sun, among dark trees, I saw the dazzle of the last rays of the sun, a sight as dramatic as the colours. Maybe a sign of hope for me on the horizon?

To the left above the striking sunset, the sky was an everyday blue. My life, as I saw it then, played out in front of me where I was standing on my balcony: while a tempest was raging inside me, for other people it was just another ordinary blue-sky day.

Four days went by during which I didn't write anything in my diary. I paged back to 22 April and read my words again, words that had meanwhile turned into flotsam. Or so it seemed to me.

It was good to read this entry again, because those four days had been tough. Waves of acute grief had washed over me. Unfortunately, those waves weren't as predictable as the tides; they just came whenever. Deep sorrow really has a way of suddenly overwhelming you, like being hit by a freak wave. It makes your knees go weak and it makes you feel like you cannot breathe. Anxiety sits like a lump in your throat.

Only much later a writer friend told me that this experience had indeed been observed. She said psychiatrist Erich Lindeman reported it in a paper on acute grief published in 1944, almost exactly as I had described it to her. According to him, a wave of pain could wash over you for 20 minutes, easily, and sometimes as long as an hour. Especially in the first weeks after Mia's death, I felt this terrible wave wash over me, but I never took note of how long this state of "drowning" lasted. Lindemann also reported that patients had told him they couldn't help sighing, and I can attest to that. This deep grief is all-consuming. You cannot do the laundry and you cannot prepare a meal. You don't want to wash your face. Actually, you don't want the sun to come up. And when it does come up, it feels like night dawning.

It's only much later that you're able to make a grocery list again, do the washing and sort of find a place for the pain outside your body.

In the days after getting the tulips I cried a little less. I started to do what had to be done. Until a wave of sorrow would catch me unawares again and knock me off my feet. Like the afternoon when I relived the accident in a very realistic flashback, especially Franché's words, "I think Miemie is gone."

I will certainly never forget the moment I realised that Mia was dead. All the dreams about the things I still wanted to experience with her, about what she would accomplish in her life, were just gone. Destroyed, like a weaver's nest.

Destination Heaven

Among the gifts of flowers and food that people brought us were what I called "consolation booklets". When you find yourself in a place of desperation, you read anything. Maybe, just maybe, among those pages you'll find an answer or a snippet that might give you solace.

I really tried to make sense of what I read. I was constantly busy arguing with myself. What could I have done differently? How could I have stopped it from happening? I relived the accident over and over in my mind.

In many of the books, the shock over a sudden death like Mia's is described accurately:

"Survivors may feel like they are wrapped in a cocoon or blanket; to others, they may look like they are holding up well. Because the reality of death has not yet penetrated awareness, survivors can appear to be quite accepting of the loss."

This quotation from *Bereavement: Reactions, Consequences, and Care* (1984) was certainly true of me. In hindsight, I realised that I'd spun myself into a cocoon. I read later that some people feel cold when they grieve the loss of a loved one. In the evenings, I would wrap myself in a blanket I'd bought years before in Clarens, that beautiful, cold little town in the Eastern Free State. I don't remember really feeling cold so much as wanting to be wrapped in that blanket...it was only autumn in Bloemfontein.

I read that researchers have observed dolphins not eating after a death in their pod. The behaviour of a greylag goose that lost its mate was described as moving about restlessly in its search, flying great distances and calling out to its lost companion, to the point of getting lost. That sounds very much like human behaviour in times of grief, and it wasn't news to me. I knew all about searching for a loved one, not eating...even forgetting to breathe.

Descriptions of people's reactions to the death of a loved one certainly rang true; about that I had no doubt. To this day I recognise those emotions and feelings.

The messages in the consolation booklets, however, gave me no consolation. I even wrote down quotes from those books in my diary in the hopes that the promises would come true.

It might have been the haze in which I moved that made those words seem meaningless. They washed over me and left me unmoved. My wound was too raw to make sense of them.

I started to read books about heaven—in fact, I amassed a small library on this subject. One book that meant a lot to me, one of the first I read, was *Heaven is for Real: A Little Boy's Astounding Story of His Trip to Heaven and Back* by Todd Burpo and Lynn Vincent.

I started to tell myself that Mia now lived somewhere else, far, yet not too far away, in a foreign country that was unreachable for the time being, but one day I'd be able to go there. That's why I started reading about that destination, just like I'd read about the places I planned to visit on my first trip to Italy, Switzerland and France. Once you start looking for them, travel guides on heaven are in ample supply. I started to read one book after the other; I just had to know what heaven looked like.

These heavenly travel guides are, obviously, mostly about near-death experiences, a topic that tends to cause raised eyebrows.

I do understand why some people have doubts about these kinds of books, but I also believe that the writers have really had such an experience. I don't think it can be proven scientifically and biblically, or biblical-scientifically (how do you separate these two, after all?). But does it matter? It remains an experience that someone had, and writing and talking about it often lead to acceptance. And that, I now know, is the most important thing. I also now know that God doesn't console everyone the same way. Perhaps you also doubt my experience of seeing Mia in her white dress on Jesus' hip. If I had had to prove my experience in a court of law, the stranger with the angel's hair in her hand would have been my only piece of evidence. To the question of whether heaven really looks like that, my response would have been a counter question: Does it really matter?

What's important is the solace I found in that first vision and the subsequent visions. And that is all that matters.

Unanswered letters

After the accident, Franché, Pauline, the boys and I all went for trauma counselling. One counsellor's suggestion was that I write a letter to the tractor driver from Stellenbosch. In the letter I wrote, among other things, that we wanted him to forgive himself, because my husband and I had already forgiven him. We had really absolved him in the spirit, because it could happen to anyone that you look and miss seeing an oncoming vehicle, and turn. Like he did on that terrible day.

I also wrote to the owner of the wine farm, trying to convey more or less the same thing, but I added that he needed to make sure his tractors were roadworthy and that the indicator lights worked. I also suggested that his staff be trained properly. I posted the letters to my sister-in-law, Ilzette, so she and Richard could deliver them to the farm in person. It was important to us to know that the letters would reach the farmer and the tractor driver.

Perhaps it was just one more thing we needed to tick off the list of things to do to prevent feelings of bitterness. I so wanted not to be angry. I wanted to walk the painful path without anger and resentment in my heart.

We never heard back from the tractor driver or his employer.

Why Mia?

Time passed.

Early in May 2013 I turned to my diary again. It was just so much easier to write than to talk.

Dear Father, today I want to come and sit at Your feet. I am utterly exhausted.

Some people are trying to make me feel better. Others behave awkwardly towards me because they themselves don't know what to do or say. Others still keep their distance; I see how they do their best to avoid running into me.

Some tell me that You picked your most beautiful flower, or that You needed a new angel. Almost as if I should feel privileged that You chose my Mia.

I think You have enough flowers, and there was no reason for You to pick "my flower". You have an entire heaven and an entire earth full of flowers!

[Here, I'd like to interrupt my diary letter to God to talk directly to you, dear reader. Please, never ever tell someone who's mourning the death of a loved one that God picks his most beautiful flowers. I have no idea where this nonsensical saying comes from. It's better to say nothing. Hug the person and say that you're praying for them. And then really pray for them, and don't stop praying.]

We'd prayed and waited for Mia for a long time, and You gave her to us. Why would You decide, after three years, to take this gift back? It doesn't make sense, Lord.

It still feels like someone is ripping my heart out of my body, every day, and throwing it on the ground.

On the one hand I feel like a woman in labour: I am exposed, and everyone is looking at me or talking about me. Some say this to me; others say that of me. Andin the meantime I'm just lying there on the maternity bed. I can't get up; I have to go through the process of labour. And if I could get up, where would I go?

I don't want to feel like this anymore, Lord.

I also don't want people telling me how long it will take me to get over it. Some say you never get over it. I believe it today, but I don't want to believe it tomorrow. If I'm never going to be happy again, someone should rather shoot me now.

I want to move through this grieving process they write about in the books. I want to complete steps 2, 3 and 4.

Some days I cry less than other days, but the suffocating feeling returns. My throat feels constricted and my breath belaboured. And when I give in and cry, then, Lord, I feel sick and nauseated.

I want to move on, but I don't really know how. Where is plan A and plan B and plan C?

Amen.

The books about heaven that I read did comfort me, simply because I knew Mia was there. But time and again the awful reality of my life here on earth without her would hit me and rip apart my very being.

Some days felt like they would never end. I wanted to notice beautiful things again without them reminding me of Mia. Everything around me made me think of her. I wanted to treasure my memories of her, but I wanted to think of her without this indescribable hurt.

Whenever I could manage to put the past and the memories to one side, the future would come knocking at my door. Then I would think of all the things Mia and I would never experience together: her first day of school, her first time falling in love, her first dance…so many things that just vanished together with her three-year existence. What was I to do with this hole, or rather the fissure, between being with the three-year-old Mia here on earth and someday being with her in Heaven?

The hole gaped…until one morning when a single pink hibiscus flower temporarily covered it up.

A pink hibiscus flower

Not long after the accident, my dear friend Ida-Marie from Johannesburg came to visit us. Our house was full of people, and it was one of those suffocating days. She arrived from the airport in a rental car, picked me up from my house of tears and people, and took me to a local nursery. She has always been my gardening friend. That morning she bought us a pink hibiscus and a beautiful pot to plant it in. We also bought a pink-leaved plum tree with one purpose: this tree had to stand out in our garden, where everything else was green. Ida-Marie returned home that same evening, little knowing that her visit would fill in a hole...if only temporarily.

Franché, the boys and I planted the hibiscus and put the pot on the balcony outside our bedroom window.

In the last week of April 2013, it flowered for the first time, shortly after my prayer about why *my* flower had had to be picked. The flowers are huge and very pink. All the other flowers that people had brought us with so much love had long since wilted. And that was as it should be, I thought, because the grim reality is that flowers that are initially so exquisite have to be thrown out once their beauty has faded.

The hibiscus flower is not everlasting either, but when she withers, she takes her leave with the promise to return. What's more, this hibiscus flower resembles my Mia in her princess outfit: the pink petals are her dress, and the stigma and anthers her crown. The potted hibiscus on our balcony became one of our first pink memorials.

A web of questions

Saturday afternoons, I discovered, were the worst. The house would be utterly quiet and I wouldn't know what to do. Franché would normally rest, and the boys would keep themselves busy. I crocheted, trying to finish the pink-and-white blanket that Mia had asked for when she was still with us, but never got. Still, the silence would overpower me.

On 4 May 2013, I wrote the following in my diary:

Lord, I know you didn't let the accident happen; it was the enemy that stole her from us. That I know.

Stéfan's friend's mother told me that he'd told her, while our mini-van was rolling, he saw a white light the entire time. He is eight years old. His words are testimony to Your presence at that accident scene, a moment I wish I could revisit and erase from history. You were really there.

Why then was Mia not spared like the rest of us?

Pauline christened her Ntswaki, a Sotho name that means "she who brings change"—such an apt name. When she arrived, the Robberts family was comprised of a dad, a mom and two sons. And Pauline.

Little did any of the five of us know exactly how much she would change our lives, with her arrival *and* with her departure.

Why did she have to go so soon? Lord, it goes against everything I believe and know of You. Lord, You have proven so many times that You are God in my life. You level uneven roads. You are especially good to us.

Your Word says You know everything that will happen in our lives, even before we were formed in the womb.

But Lord...couldn't You have prevented this one? Lord God, did I do something wrong? God, I don't understand.

Did I have to suffer such terrible pain so that I could do some good for Your kingdom? It's like something alien; it just doesn't fit in the picture I have of You, of me and of this world.

Many more words, phrases and sentences like these flowed from my pen on that day in June. Nearly all of them ended with question marks. No full stops. In places, an exclamation mark too, signifying desperation.

Here's how I ended one of these May letters to God:

Lord, touch me with Your Spirit so that all these questions will melt away. God, flood me with Your love and grace and peace. Show me Your sadness so that it can make sense to me.

Lord, only You can fill the hole in my heart with Your Spirit. Nothing else.

Lord, forgive me for saying things that hurt Your heart. Forgive me for those days when I'm uncertain about the fact that You are always in control.

I lay all this anger and hurt and questions I have inside me at Your feet, because I am tired.

I only want to experience peace. I want to know that Mia is with You, and I want to be okay with that.

Amen.

On 5 May 2013 I woke up after another night of dreaming, this time a very confusing dream. I'd dreamt that Mia had been murdered and that we'd held a funeral for her, but a few days later she was with us again, alive. We hugged her and kissed her and held her tightly.

It felt so good to have her with us. She slept up against me and, in my dream, when it was time to get up I fetched her Bambi school uniform to help her dress. We were planning to tell everyone at Bambi the good news, but then I realised I shouldn't take Mia back to school because it would just confuse the other toddlers. The dream made it clear to me that Mia wasn't back for good; she'd just come for a visit because she was now living elsewhere. I couldn't interpret the dream, but it felt wonderful to have felt her presence again. The dream reassured me in a way.

I wrote down these passages from the Amplified Bible in my diary; I didn't have words of my own.

[1]"...I have called you by your name; you are Mine!

[2]"When you pass through the waters, I will be with you;

And through the rivers, they will not overwhelm you.

When you walk through the fire, you will not be scorched,

Nor will the flame burn you.

[3]"For I am the Lord your God..."

– Isaiah 43: 1–3

[1]He who dwells in the shelter of the Most High

Will remain secure *and* rest in the shadow of the Almighty [whose power no enemy can withstand].

[2]I will say of the Lord, "He is my refuge and my fortress,

My God, in whom I trust [with great confidence, and on whom I will rely)!"

[3]For He will save you from the trap of the fowler,

And from the deadly pestilence.

[4]He will cover you *and* completely protect you with His opinions,

And under His wings you will find refuge;

His faithfulness is a shield and a wall.

[5]You will not be afraid of the terror of night,

Nor of the arrow that flies by day...

[11]For He will command His angels in regard to you,

To protect *and* defend *and* guard you in all your ways [of obedience and service].

– Psalm 91:1–5, 11

Question marks

It was still May. I spoke to my uncle, Oom[1] Gerrie. Someone needed to help me free myself from this web of whys and questions about God. Day in and day out, I spun my web, but the only prey likely to get ensnared was me.

I was struggling to connect with God, to reach Him. Had I become so entangled in my web and even paralysed by venom that I had become deaf and blind to Him?

Oom Gerrie talked to me gently. I remember phrases such as, "God mourns with you" and "God is not punishing you." I felt better for a while, but then the questions returned. If she had been buckled up during the accident, could the outcome have been different?

"We will never know," Oom Gerrie said.

I had to resign myself to this fact. That's just how it was.

It was over.

I started an argument with myself...or was it Oom Gerrie who'd asked the counter questions? Either way, I filled pages of my diary that evening. Again, sentences with question marks, and no full stops or exclamation marks.

Is it similar to how God didn't stop Adam and Eve from eating the forbidden fruit? He had given them—and me—free will in this life; couldn't he have stopped me from not buckling Mia up?

Or what about David, a man after God's own heart, who committed adultery and then his infant son died? And what about Paul and the other loyal apostles who were tortured? Couldn't God have stopped any one of these things from happening?

---

1. Afrikaans for Mr.

That evening, I again reminded myself that nowhere in the Bible does God promise that bad thing won't ever happen to us. What He does promise is that He would always be with us. I went to sleep with these thoughts in my head.

Now, when I look back, I know that even Jesus was tested by the devil when he told Him to jump off the roof of the temple to prove that the angels would save Him (Luke 4). Jesus said no to this challenge; He knew there was no guarantee that the angels would catch Him.

Somewhere in May, the threads of the web started to loosen their grip. There was mercy, after all, on that terrible day in March. I made a list:

• The rest of us weren't seriously injured.
• Mia went straight to heaven.
• She didn't suffer.
• She hadn't been afraid.
• She hadn't been injured so badly that she would never walk again. I can't imagine how such a livewire could have sat still.
• We didn't see her die.
• She spent the last moment of her life on earth in my arms.
• As she lay there on the grass next to the road, she looked beautiful, perfect and at peace.

The picture of my little girl on the grass kept running through my head relentlessly. At least it was *this* picture and not one of a mutilated girl, something for which I was grateful.

It was as if I could start to think rationally. The fog of emotions started to lift here and there so that I could begin to see the awful, cold facts of that day too. People had made mistakes: the tractor driver who could or would not use his indicator; Mia sitting in the most dangerous place in the car, without a safety belt. Her injuries were just too severe.

A covenant

It was autumn when I sat in my room one day, praying. My eyes were closed, and I saw myself sitting at Jesus' feet.

Jesus was sitting on a throne. I saw His white robe; no, I *touched* it. I felt my body resting heavily against His legs. All around me there was light. Everything was bright—like the sea shimmering in the sunlight, not like a disco ball's glittering reflections. I heard voices: it sounded like people laughing, but the sound came from outside. In the room where I sat at Jesus' feet, it was only Him and me. I called for Franché and Stéfan and Morné, and the next moment they were there too. Jesus' one hand rested on Franché's shoulder, and with His other hand he stroked the boys' hair. He smiled at us. Then His hand was on my head. Our family wrapped our arms around each other, forming a circle. To an onlooker it must have looked like a glowing circle. I felt something flow through us.

I didn't know it then, but I realised later that this was solace and healing.

It was so powerful that I also called Pauline and Montsheng, Pauline's youngest daughter who lived with us, to this healing room. They joined us in the circle because they're part of our daily family life.

The feeling of warmth remained inside me. I also saw Mia outside this bright room. She was playing in a garden and she had a look of contentment on her face. One by one, Pauline and Tshengie took the two boys out of the room. Jesus still had His arms around Franché and me. He embraced us more closely, forming a small, tight circle. The sensation of something flowing through us intensified. We looked each other in the eye and we knew: this circle was unbreakable. And that's how it would remain.

What happened that morning, I later saw as a kind of covenant. The message was clear: our strength lies in Jesus, but also in each other.

If it were a Hollywood movie, Franché and I would have walked off into the sunset hand in hand. But it wasn't. What happened was something far greater than Hollywood's best, and it shone more brightly than all the gold Oscar statues together.

Nothing would ever separate us from each other or from Jesus.

Rainbow

Her absence is like the sky, spread over everything.
– C.S. Lewis, A Grief Observed

Life goes on.

Just before winter set in, we went away with friends to their game farm near Griekwastad in the Northern Cape—our first trip as a family without Mia.

It was exceptionally quiet on the farm.

I miss you, Mia, I said to the wind. I miss your open-mouthed smile, your exuberant laughter and your chatter. You would have been crazy about the lambs that the boys got to pat.

That Sunday was Mother's Day, another first I had to get through. The previous night I got my Mother's Day gift: a dream about Mia. I don't remember the details—I didn't write down my dream after waking up as I would have done at home—but she was there.

I thanked Jesus.

We listened to music in the car on our way home, and the song "Until I'm Home" by Nianell came up in the playlist. I saw tears running down Stéfan's cheeks. Morné was fast asleep. Franché and I wept, this time less for our own loss and more because our eldest was crying and missing his sister.

That evening we lit a pink sky lantern and set it adrift in the field near our house. The sun disappeared in a sea of pink. The crescent moon hung in the heavens, and a bright star flickered next to it. It was Mia, we all thought.

In the weeks after the pink sunset I again experienced the heart-to-heart with Jesus in the throne room. On one occasion He offered me water, which was ice-cold and tasted almost sweet. The experience was so real that I could taste the water in my mouth.

I cried less, but the longing intensified. One day, when the longing again pierced me like a dagger, I went to sit in my room. Jesus greeted me as I closed my eyes, from which the tears had been rolling uncontrollably that morning. I sensed that He was going to show me something very special. And then she came running into the room. It felt like a surprise party for me!

Mia ran into my arms. I felt her little body against mine, and her soft hair against my cheek. I wondered how it could feel that real. My hands moved from her shoulders to her middle; everything was tangible.

"Be good here with Jesus," I told her.

"I really enjoy it here," she responded. Her blue eyes were full of life and her mouth was laughing, but she wasn't being frivolous. She was actually quieter than usual. Maybe she missed me too, I thought. I got a hug from her. I felt content; that's what I'd needed that day.

For the first time I sensed that Mia perhaps felt sorry for me, and that she wanted to tell me that she was happy in her new home. When she ran out of the room, which had by now become familiar to me, I felt a big hand on my shoulder. Jesus held me. He knew how much I was yearning to hold her little body in my arms again.

He knew absolutely.

In the last week of May, 2013, I realised that two months had passed since our little Miemie left us.

Sometimes it felt as if I was doing better. There were days when I didn't cry at all. But there were still days when I thought, surely everything had been just a horrible dream?

Exactly two months after Mia's death I wrote her name and the date in my Bible next to Psalm 30:

[5] ...Weeping may endure for a night,
But a shout of joy comes in the morning.
[11] You have turned my mourning into dancing for me;
You have taken off my sackcloth and clothed me with joy.

Sometime in June 2013, I came to understand that this was now the new normal: the fact that Mia was gone had become reality. This realisation didn't prevent me, however, from going to meet Jesus.

One morning I was again struggling to get images of the accident scene out of my head. I sat down in my special place and in my mind's eye I saw her earthly body lying still on the grass. As I was hoping that she was unconscious only, I saw things I hadn't noticed on the day of the accident: her tummy was flat and wrinkled (a sign that the breath had left her body, I now know), her neck was in an unnatural position, and her skin was an odd colour (without the pink undertone that I knew). And then, suddenly, there was a script change in the scene that had been running through my head.

I witnessed how Mia climbed out of her body and I saw Jesus standing there. He picked her up and held her. I saw myself running around on the accident scene, just like I had on that day, and I saw Franché in his blue shirt kneeling next to her body. He was crying.

Why was I only seeing these things now?

I also saw how Jesus and Mia moved away from us. He held her head against His chest. He didn't want her to see her dad in his blue shirt crying, or her mom running around hysterically, or her brother with a nosebleed. He took her away.

She wasn't crying. I knew she was already experiencing the supernatural peace that had filled her once her last breath had left her body. What a relief it was to know she was safe.

I saw her and Jesus sitting down on a bench in a beautiful garden with big green trees and birds singing. I also saw Mari again—my friend who had had three sons here on earth but who, just like me, had longed for a little girl. Mari never got the daughter she wanted in her time of being a mother here on earth, before she left us for heaven too soon. While Jesus was talking to Mia (it looked as if He was explaining something to her), Mari stepped closer to them. She looked at Jesus reverently, and she seemed to nod as He talked. Then she was talking to Mia.

Perhaps she was explaining to Mia who she was, and that she knew her mommy and daddy well. Mia's face seemed to brighten when she heard our names.

She slipped off Jesus' lap and walked over to a group of children. At first she stood aside and smiled at the jokes they were making. One child took Mia's hand and pulled her into the circle. Together they whirled round and round, and they were laughing. Sitting to one side, Jesus and Mari were still talking. I sensed that Jesus was telling Mari how she could help Mia here in her new home. The colour of the light was slowly changing, as if dusk was falling, although it remained a warm colour. It looked like it does when clouds pass in front of the sun on a hot day in Bloemfontein. I saw how everyone started to move away in different directions, like they always did whenever I was granted this vision of heaven. I knew it had become time to say goodbye. Mia didn't walk away on her own; Mari was holding her hand. It looked as if they were talking. Mia smiled shyly, and I realised she knew enough and understood enough about this new place and why we weren't there yet.

I had this experience in June 2013, but it would take me many years—until 30 October 2017—before I wrote about it in this book. On that day I smelled Mia. To make sure that I was not imagining it, I smelled a number of objects, even myself, to eliminate all other possibilities. Every time I started to write about that memory, the scent of the cheap perfume that Mia used to love spraying on herself would fill the room.

In the throne-room visits that followed, I regularly saw little children sitting with Jesus. He would stroke their hair and hug them. It looked as if they waited for Him every day, and He always showed up.

One suitcase fewer

That winter holiday we travelled to Mozambique in search of the sun's heat. On the beach in Inhambane I read a book about heaven. I read about terrible things, among others a piece about Jesus' death on the cross. One phrase in particular struck me deeply: "blood and tears concealed His eyes of love". When I looked up from the pages of

the book, I saw a little blonde-haired girl running on the beach. An overwhelming feeling of gratitude welled up in me. Thank you, Lord, I said. Thank you that Mia is with you in paradise. And thank you for the sacrifice Your Son made so that Mia—and me with her—could have eternal life.

Later that afternoon, the boys and I went for a walk on the beach. Words seemed to flow easier for them here by the sea. They asked me about Mia and where she was, and how we could be so sure of it. I explained many things to them—things you never thought you'd have to explain to your children at such a young age.

I also told them that all babies and little children go to heaven. We talked about the fact that children reach an age when they could decide whether they wanted to serve the Lord or not. My two sons were very eager to choose the Lord, and right there on the beach in a foreign country, far from everything, we prayed together and my two sons voluntarily chose to accept the Lord as their God the Father and Jesus as their Saviour.

The seaside holiday in Mozambique was our first one without Mia. Thinking back, the thing that struck me most was that I had one fewer suitcase to pack.

On the way to our destination, during an overnight stop in Komatipoort, I cried myself to sleep because of that one suitcase we hadn't needed to bring. But, in Mozambique, the sunsets were pinker than ever. No camera could capture it properly. That's where I realised that God's comfort would follow me wherever I went. Dusk after dusk I experienced his presence.

My messy house

For months my home was really messy. I had no strength or desire to open and tidy cupboards or drawers, because whatever I opened, there Mia was. More than three months later I still wasn't ready to let go of her and her belongings.

When I finally started in July, it was with clay that had hardened slightly but was still pliable. I gave it to Vinci, a playmate of Mia's and the son of the grounds man at Bambi Pre-Primary. For both Vinci and me, this second-hand clay was like gold.

In my office, I took every paintbrush, every art project and every shredded piece of paper in my hands. It was extremely difficult. With every reminder I said goodbye, over and over. The hurt inside me didn't have time to fester because it kept pouring out.

My Mia file, in which I kept her best artworks, report cards and certificates of extramural activities, also now contained her death certificate.

It was difficult to file it, but it helped me that day to accept that I was not going to wake from this dream. It would be the first document I saw whenever I opened her file.

A while later I opened the school career album I'd ordered before the accident and filled it with all the photographs of Mia's short school career. There were many photos of concerts, water fun days and other occasions. The album that was meant for 12 school years was now filled with three-and-a-half years' memories. It's another memorial that's like a jewel to me.

After the first week's attempts to tidy my house, I called a halt for the time being. I decided that on this journey there were no shoulds and should nots; I would eat the elephant one bite at a time.

I didn't see my way clear to deal with Mia's room and wardrobe yet.

In the meantime, I'd also decided that I'd like to give everything of Mia's that was still useful to people who'd known her rather than throw it in the bin or give it to people who'd have no idea how difficult it was for me to give her things away. I realised that I was searching for a purpose in this tidying process.

Could death be God's grace?

On Sunday, 14 July 2013, I wrote the following in my diary:

Thank you, Lord, that even the most horrible memory of Mia is still a beautiful picture. The injuries she sustained in the accident were to the back of her head. I saw the wound and I saw some of her brain tissue on the grass. But her expression was calm and peaceful. There was not even a scratch on her face. She was not mutilated. She was as beautiful as ever.

Looking back now, I know that if Mia had survived the accident, she would have been severely disabled. And for that busy bee with her blonde hair, big blue eyes, nimble body and exuberant laughter it would have been devastating if she'd been paralysed. It would have been too distressing for us too. Her older brother Stéfan said, "But, Mom, if she had lived and it had been like this, our sadness would have never ended."

If I'd had a choice...I also would have chosen for her to rather go to heaven and to live there fully like the little girl she was here on earth.

As long as our children were happy, we were happy. That's all that mattered. We as parents would cope with whatever...

In my story there was grace for me. It's something I say with the utmost respect, because I know there are people whose circumstances differ from mine.

The firm knowledge that Mia was having a wonderful time in heaven and had experienced no suffering was a solace that made this difficult journey more bearable.

The prospect of seeing her again, that's what kept me going, and what kept me at God's feet.

I knew that the enemy's master plan included causing separation between me and my God after this traumatic event. Marriages break down and people get angry at other people or, worse yet, at God. Because they are under the illusion that God controls everything on our life's journey.

Why then do bad things still happen? Isn't God in control of everything?

No, He is not. We live in an imperfect world where many things can go wrong. People make wrong choices and disasters hit randomly. We live in a world where the enemy is in charge. If you don't believe me, just watch the news, local as well as international news. God is the God of love. Somewhere in the Bible it says that if you ask the Lord for a loaf of bread, He will not give you a stone. What it does *not* say is that if the Lord has given you the bread, He will after three years decide to take it back. God is only love. He cannot deny himself and be something other than love. So the concept of a God that "takes back" or "sends disease" or "allows bad things to happen" goes against every biblical principle and the nature of our Heavenly Father. He gives. That's what He does. And He loves. That's what He is made of: love.

No disease, accident, disabled child, sudden death, cancer or anything else that causes pain is God's plan for your life. He does not send bad things. And He does not allow bad things to happen. He does not test your faith. He does not try to draw you closer to Him through such bad experiences. God only wants to love you. He only wants the best for you.

'For I know the plans and thoughts that I have for you,' says the Lord, 'plans for peace and well-being and not for disaster, to give you a future and a hope.'

– Jeremiah 29:11

The Lord's heart breaks when we are hurt. Thank you, Lord, for the grace in this.

We must choose to detect grace in our difficult circumstances because it is always present. We just have to be on the lookout for it.

For us as a family, our experiences of Jesus' infinite love sometimes happened in the strangest places. At other times it was obvious why I experienced God in that place or that moment. Like the day when, after an appointment, I was driving back home on the south side of Bloemfontein. One of the imaginary boundaries between the north and the south of our small city is the so-called Show Bridge. As I was driving across the bridge, something that looked different than usual caught my eye. It took me a moment or two to realise that new barriers had been erected on either side of the bridge; they were so new that they were still shiny. The next moment my mind flashed back to the accident. The barriers were looking so solid, but they're not. My train of thought went to the barrier next to Bottelary Road, and the ease with which our minivan had smashed through it.

In my mind's eye I relived the accident right there in my car. I recalled every second of it. But I also saw that Jesus really knew of everything that has happened to us on our path of life, including the wrong choices and the hurt. I saw that, at the precise moment that bad things happen to us, He as good as closes His eyes and holds His breath, because here it comes...the Robberts family's tragedy is about to happen. I sensed His deep compassion for us, His children, when we get hurt. The imperfect world also pains Him. In those moments as I was driving across the Show Bridge with its shiny barriers, I had a profound experience of Jesus' compassion for us in a world where things happen over which He has no control.

That little body...

On 23 July 2013—a difficult day—I wrote the following in my diary:

My heart aches with longing.

Yesterday evening, I attended the boys' choir festival performance. A family with a little blonde-haired girl sat down next to me. Out of the corner of my eye I saw her fidgeting and playing to entertain herself. I tried hard not to look at her, but I couldn't get her out of my field of vision. Finally, I forced myself to look directly at her to convince myself: Look, it's not Mia. It's a little girl I don't know. She peered shyly at me.

It didn't help.

I missed my daughter's little body tucked into my side. I remembered exactly how she felt when I touched her: her body was plump, and softer than her brothers' bodies.

I remembered exactly how she smelled—when she'd just had a bath and smelled baby clean, but also when, after a hot day, she'd come to sit with me with her sweaty little body. I remembered what her hair felt like between my fingers. I missed everything about her so much!

For a long time, if I had to drive somewhere, it felt to me that I was forgetting something. I had a mental checklist: did I have my phone, my keys, my handbag, my jacket, the boys and all their things? Still, the niggle would remain: something was missing. And then I'd realise that it was Mia's absence I was feeling. A piece of me was missing.

I hoped that, in time, the feeling would fade.

That morning, I again entered my inner room to cry at Jesus' feet. Sobs racked my body. I felt how Jesus held me tightly; He shared my pain.

Then I felt His strong hands wiping the tears from my cheeks. The flood of tears lessened. He folded his hand around my heart; it really felt as if His hand reached all the way into my chest and took my heart and held it.

In His eyes I saw sincere, heartfelt pity for me, and I experienced His infinite love for me.

He knew the pain of a broken heart.

He put His other hand on mine and His fingers slipped between mine so he could hold my hand tightly.

And he said, "Hold on. It's going to be okay. Just hang in there. It *will* get better."

I experienced Him showing me how to breathe deeply. I could inhale some of His power, or of His spirit, or of His solace. Something precious. My body slowly calmed down and I stopped shaking.

Like a roller-coaster

During the months after the accident many people told Franché and me that we had to take care of our marriage. I'd already asked people who were at Mia's memorial service to keep praying for us and for our marriage, because I had heard the warnings by then.

You're aware of the need to do this, but you also wrestle with your own emotions to such an extent that you simply have too little energy left over to work on your relationship.

Franché and I had already forgiven each other a day or so after the accident and had vowed never to point a finger at each other. But we had to do this over and over, or at least remind each other of the day we sat on that fallen tree trunk and said we would never blame each other.

Franché walked his own path through grief. He is not fond of holding a conversation (as he calls it) about Mia's death, or anything else. Quietly and on his own, he mourned his daughter.

The two of us walked together, but actually we were each on our own path and walked it at our own pace. Some days he was up and I was down. On the days when he was down, I was up again. Just like a roller-coaster.

Yes, there were times when I was seriously frustrated with his way of mourning. And he certainly with mine too. But how can you judge another person's way of dealing with pain?

While I just wanted to make memorials for Mia, he kept working harder. It made me feel like I wanted to remember and he wanted to forget. It simply hurt so much that he rather wanted to forget.

Years before, when we had begun to hope for a little girl, I started to plant pink flowers and buy pink clothes. To think that I had always thought of myself as more of a blue girl! While Mia was here with us, she and I indulged in everything pink.

After she left us, I started to plant lots of pink flowers in the garden again, and trees that bore pink flowers. It was part of my celebration of the extraordinary pink times with my Mia.

You're often confronted with the various theories about grief, especially when you yourself are going through the process of grieving. Steps that you apparently have to go through. There might be certain stages and steps that apply generally, but I certainly did not experience the "proposed order". What I do know is that the months after Mia's death were the most turbulent and confusing emotional ride ever.

I read somewhere about cope mode, aggression, outbursts, and a deep grieving phase. I also read that, after the death of a child, the father and the mother are probably never together in the same stage of grief.

This is true, but in a way it is a mercy. When you're laid low, your partner is okay. And vice versa.

During that first year I mostly felt insecure—simply because I never knew which emotions were going to hit me.

Knowing what I know now, that was okay: you have to take it as it comes. If you want to cry and stay in bed, do it. If you don't feel like talking to anyone about how you're feeling, then don't. I just had to take care that I didn't keep doing the same thing, like staying in bed every day or only focusing on doing charity work.

Whatever I did, one golden thread ran through everything: I had to remain close to God—whether I was at the top, in the middle or at the bottom of the roller-coaster of loss.

"Dance me to the end of love"

One Saturday evening in August 2013, good friends of ours, Hettie and Gys, invited us over for supper. Gys, who loves music, at one point took his daughter Rentia by the hand and, to the beat of a catchy song, twirled her around the room a few times.

I could see and I could sense that moment when Gys's dancing with his daughter ripped my husband's heart out of his body. I didn't know what went through his mind, but in my mind's eye I saw him, also a music aficionado, holding Mia and dancing to the Kurt Darren song "Kaptein" ("Patyn", as she pronounced it).

It was their song. And he would never, ever again be able to dance with his daughter to that song.

We went home early that evening.

The following week, in the room of healing, Jesus showed me Franché and Mia holding each other again. They were dancing, and laugh lines creased from the corners of his eyes.

Leonard Cohen sings:

Dance me to your beauty with a burning violin,

Dance me through the panic till I'm gathered safely in,

Lift me like an olive branch and be my homeward dove,

Dance me to the end of love,

Dance me to the end of love.

Only years after Mia's death did Franché write about the worst day of his life for the first time. (Read the chapter "When a Father Mourns.")

(Super)natural phenomena

I know the sun sets every day, just as it rises every day. There is something reassuring about this fact. But some days a sunrise or a sunset can be more special than on other days.

About two months after Mia's death, I started to experience God's nearness to me in sunsets specifically. It often happened on my "down" days. Do you look at nature differently when you're feeling down? Or does God communicate with us in a different way on such days? Is it perhaps always there and we just don't notice it?

I'd read somewhere that "chance"—such as the sun by chance setting in a pink blaze on a very bad day—can be described as a small miracle when God chooses to remain anonymous. Even though this explanation has no literary depth or clever pun, I find it valuable. I saw an incredible number of natural wonders by chance in the months and years after Mia's death. I wrote about some of them during that terrible 2013:

On my balcony hangs a heart cut out of tin. Inside the heart there is an angel. It was a gift from someone who was at Mia's memorial service. On the morning of 6 June 2013, the sun's rays bounced off the tin heart and reflected a distinct heart against my bedroom window. Random, yes, but I happened to be in my room at that fleeting moment. I couldn't miss it.

While we were on holiday in Mozambique, my dear friend Carla decorated the hibiscus pot on our balcony with mosaics. She and I had bought the tiles together. This pot was meant to be a memorial to Mia. On the morning of 26 June 2013, she sent me a photo of the memorial in the making: everywhere she'd applied glue, everywhere her hands had touched, even in the shadow behind the pot, there were tiny rainbows.

On an ordinary morning in July 2013, the 21st, to be exact, I was walking to the kitchen when I saw a rainbow in the corridor near the children's bedrooms. I walked into Mia's bedroom, and there the same rainbow illuminated the rug. I knew I could attribute the phenomenon to the glass balustrades in our house that reflected the sun from outside. But during this year it happened more often than it ever did before. It was as if the sun didn't want to leave us alone. The play of light had become a form of therapy for me.

On the morning of 5 September 2013, the regular rainbow phenomenon found its way into my sanctuary—my inner room. It was huge and vivid. If felt as if the rainbow had come to fetch me from my refuge where I'd been hiding from the world.

And then, on 6 October 2013, just before 4 o'clock in the afternoon, I saw a rainbow at the back of our house, the shady side, for the very first time. Next to the dog kennel it hung clear as day, while the sun was already on the far west side of the house. Even in a neglected corner of our garden, I experienced God's nearness.

We'd been holidaying in Ballito for seven years. Our holiday home there was full of memories of Mia. Mia on the beach, Mia sleeping with us in the king-size bed, Mia with her two brothers. Our seaside holiday in December 2013 was our first one without her. In all the years that we'd been going to Ballito, I'd never seen a rainbow there. Rain on the KwaZulu-Natal North Coast is not usually accompanied by dramatic thunderstorms and spectacular rainbows afterwards. That changed in December 2013. We saw a giant rainbow touching the sea, and it was as if the ends of that rainbow had come to tie off this *annus horribilis* for us as a family.

The ultimate in rainbow miracles, however, happened on 1 November 2013, when I took *another* photo of *another* remarkable rainbow from our porch. On the same day I received a photo from Carla, my friend who'd decorated the hibiscus pot with mosaics. This photo had been taken by her cousin, who regularly drove along Bottelary Road, where our minivan had rolled and Mia had died. It took a long time for the photo to download on my phone.

And then I saw it: an image of the most beautiful rainbow, taken earlier that afternoon. Nearly 1 000 km from me, the same rainbow arced in the sky.

I felt as if I were floating.

Dark

Sometimes, happy memories hurt the most.
– Unknown

A party without her

Mia was born on 12 August.

On 6 August 2013 I started to organise a celebration of her fourth birthday, her first one away from us. A few friends and I had decided to have the party at a local children's home in the hope that my terrible heartache could at least make a few other hearts happy. Making all the arrangements did help to distract me, but somewhere amid the flurry of activity the reality hit me that Mia would not come skipping along at any moment.

While I was planning Mia's party without Mia, I started to feel like she might have been just a dream, as if I had never had a daughter by the name of Mia. Could something—worse yet, someone who'd been real—fade away from memory so quickly? It hit me that the double-edged sword of such deep loss cut both ways: as the pain of knowing she wasn't here with us any more dulled, the loss of memories pierced my heart all over again.

It's a little like an overseas holiday: you remember specifics for a long time, like what and where you ate, what the hotel room looked like and how much you paid for a cool drink. But later, when you look at the photos again, you realise that you've forgotten the details, because in your memory bank you only have space for the main thoughts: the Arc de Triomph, the Eiffel Tower, Big Ben...

It's painful to realise that letting go and getting better also sometimes mean forgetting. Actually, it's not only painful but also cruel. But it's also a process you cannot stop.

On the Monday morning of her birthday, a few days before the party, I found myself back in the throne room. Jesus held me while I lay with my head on His legs. He consoled me. He understood the pain of forgetting and remembering.

I saw Mia again. She was wearing a white dress with a bright-pink sash, and she radiated light. There was a glow around her pale-white porcelain-doll face. "Hi, Mom," she said.

She held out the most beautiful pink flowers to me. They looked exactly like the pink cyclamens blooming outside our bedroom window. The stems of the flowers were hanging untidily between her plump fingers. She smiled at me and held out her arms while still holding the flowers in one hand. (As I put this experience down on paper, I could see her little hands in my mind's eye again. They were so distinct that day, her hands.)

I took the flowers from her, picked her up and held her against me in a long, tight hug—a hug like only Mia could give. She gave me a big kiss. I felt her lips against mine. Then I stepped back. I saw her widening her eyes, like she always used to do. Then she burst out laughing. "Love you, Mom!" she said excitedly.

She turned around, took Mari's hand and walked away. She looked content and happy.

She had brought me flowers to lighten the terrible longing in my heart.

Thank you, Jesus.

On the Saturday morning of Mia's birthday party, just before I had to leave home, I had a quiet time in my usual place in my room. I saw her again.

She was excited and was skipping around the garden. She was playing with her friends. It was as if she knew that this was her special day. Her white dress seemed to have a pink tinge, but her face was still pale white and soft.

I told her I wished I could stay there all day and just watch her, but I excused myself with a sudden thought, not knowing if I said it out loud: "You know what it's like, with us here and you there. And you're okay with it. I know that. So I'm okay with it too. Your face is radiating a wisdom—or perhaps contentment—well beyond your years."

At the children's home my friends and I gave each little girl a princess outfit that we'd made ourselves: a cloak, a skirt, a pink sash and a crown. We made up the girls faces and painted their nails. We gave them party packets containing snacks. It was just like an ordinary children's party, with one exception: the birthday girl wasn't there.

Still, we ate pink cupcakes.

Later, I realised it definitely helped me to survive that first big day without her, and many more after that. The big days creep up on you until they hover over you like a big shadow. I knew my friends and I made a difference that day—even if it was to ease my own pain, and even though, afterwards, I lay on my bed, holding my pillow, and cried until I had no tears left.

Mia's grandfather

Soon after the party at the children's home my dad came to visit us. It had been almost a year since his stroke. He was not the same man I knew before. My father had become slow-witted, he struggled to read and he could not express himself properly.

The last time he saw Mia at our house in Bloemfontein was during the school holiday in September 2012, not long after he'd had the stroke. He was fragile and self-conscious. To Mia, however, he was still just her grandpa. She was the only one who had no problem communicating with him. The two of them sat for hours talking, exchanging clearly understandable, gentle words. I have a vague memory of Mia and her grandpa sitting in the sun in perfect harmony.

This was his first time being at our house without Mia there. His understanding was limited, but I could see he didn't know how to express his emotions over Mia's death. He was also hurting—hurting over Mia and certainly also hurting over what was happening to him.

One afternoon during his visit, when the low sun was shining into the living room, I talked to him about heaven. I told him about my heavenly encounters with Mia over the past few months. His outlook on this kind of thing had always been conservative. That, and his condition, made it a difficult conversation. Yet I was able to convince him of the reality that we would see her, and our other loved ones, again...because we believed in Jesus.

This was an unlikely conversation to have had with my dad. To talk to him about faith, let alone praying together, had never been part of our relationship. And here, soon after the rewarding party at the children's home, it happened.

Both of these miraculous events stemmed from Mia's death.

I closed off August with gratitude for these two events. Even if it was only for that. Up to that point.

Mia's brothers

Stéfan and Morné also navigated their own path of grief. I know now that I was so consumed by my own grief that I sometimes missed seeing theirs. We did take them for regular therapy sessions soon after the accident. The therapist frequently said Stéfan admitted his pain and talked about it, but Morné was reticent. That was what we noticed at home too. Maybe it was because Stéfan was two years older? They were only 8 and 6 years old at the time of the accident. After one session the therapist told me that Morné sometimes secretively went to Mia's room to play with her toys, and there he would weep quietly about the loss of his little sister. It broke my heart to hear it. It took me a while to realise that we were all mourning in our own way and at our own pace, and that we had to leave it at that. In the end I couldn't do much more for my sons than give their broken hearts to the Lord.

Spring arrived

My diary entry on 9 September 2013 read as follows:

I miss her with all my being. Sometimes the longing is unbearable. At other times the fact that she's gone feels unreal.

I find that little things are starting to fade from memory, whereas other things stick in my mind.

Every time before a meal when I stand in front of the cupboard in which we keep the crockery, I hear her voice: "The pink bowl, Mommy, I want the pink bowl." This always happened, no matter what we ate. And now, with every single meal, I hear her say it. Whenever Franché and I went out for a date night, she always waited for us, sleeping on the brown leather sofa under the loving care of Pauline. The little pale body formed a contrast against the dark-brown leather. I have the memories of picking her up and carrying her to her bed. When we get home now, I look at the sofa and I see her pale body lying there, even though the sofa is empty and dark.

Over weekends, the silence overwhelms me. I feel I have to keep myself busy, but my body is weary. Crocheting has gradually become my refuge. I crochet all the time. It is a slight source of frustration for my husband, since I've become less and less involved in the household, but I don't know what else to do.

Most of the time I do not want to be here. I do not want to go through this. I want to run away. But where to? The pain follows me everywhere I go.

The realisation that Mia isn't here anymore crops up at every turn, near and far from home. I cannot avoid it. People tell me I shouldn't be in a rush to get through the grieving process. Sometimes I think, I now want to cry for days so I can just get it over with. Is that what they mean? If you mourn enough, are you working through the process?

Do you ever finish mourning?

Some days it feels as if life goes on as usual. I organise everything for the school bazaar's pancake stand, just like last year. I help the boys with their homework, and then another week has passed.

I remember wondering one day, if I just stood here and screamed, screamed very loudly, might the pain burst forth from my heart like a lanced abscess?

Your body and mind and life move on, but your heart doesn't follow.

I find that I am intensely focused on other's people's pain. The news is full of stories about rape and children being abused—and every snippet catches my eye. Reports of car accidents—I read them all. When I hear an ambulance siren, I writhe with pain. And then, as an antidote to my own pain, I start praying for the people involved. I try to forget how I felt when the ambulance was on its way to the hospital with us on that awful day.

Every time I read about a freak accident or a child who has died of cancer, I develop a burning desire to go and help the people deal with their pain. I feel I want to help people whose children had been hurt, but I also realise that nothing can help. I myself am still on this terrible journey. I can barely help myself, but I want to help others. Is it to forget about my own pain?

When I later read a diary entry like this one, I realised there would come a day when I'd be grateful for the time that had passed and the amount of tears I'd shed from that first day of my loss. I almost felt as if I'd achieved something. I realise how strange this may seem to you reading this. Could grief—and the different stages of grief—then be described as an achievement? Could one be grateful for such a thing?

Throughout it all—the questions as well as, I dare say, the growth—I continued to make memorials for Mia. I planted trees with pink blossoms and I planted pink flowers. When spring arrived in Bloemfontein, everything started to bloom. It was only pink flowers I saw everywhere.

And sometimes I only saw little blonde-haired girls, like at the school bazaar in October 2013.

The previous year, Mia went with me to her brothers' bazaar, or *kermis*[1]. She'd dubbed it "*krismis.*" She was, of course, not far off. A bazaar is a lot like Christmas: there is much organising, no one wants to be excluded, people get mad at each other, and everyone eats too much. Still, it is delightful. Sometime during the course of the warm spring day I went looking for my sons on the rugby field to apply some sunscreen to their faces. My eyes searched for them, but every little blond-haired girl I saw interrupted the search right there. That day, the pain suffocated me. Her voice calling me among the hubbub of all the children made me choke.

Soon, I would have to tackle the real Christmas without her. Would that also turn into a milestone? In some of the consolation books, working through all the firsts is described as a milestone. A milestone? Really? Are milestones not things that one *wants* to achieve?

And yet, one becomes grateful for the abhorrent milestones.

The day after the suffocating school bazaar, I wrote the following prayer, actually, a plea, in my diary:

---

1. A fair or carnival, especially one held to raise money for a charity.

Lord God, only You have the answer. Lord, only You can help me and make things better for me. If it's at all possible. Just be with me and fill me with Your spirit, because I don't know any more.

Why, when and how? I really don't know anything.

"Majesty, Majesty, Your grace has found me just as I am, empty-handed but alive in Your hands" [words from the lyrics of the song "Majesty" by the English Christian band Delirious].

Lord God, I do not know what to ask, because I do not know where I am, where I want to be, or how to get there.

I only know I do not want to feel the way I am feeling now. I feel trapped. Help me. Forgive me.

Stéfan turned nine that spring. God's gift to me on my eldest's birthday was a special encounter in the throne room—even before his birthday.

I saw Stéfan standing tall and alone in front of Jesus in his throne room. Jesus anointed him. Our whole family stood together and held each other close, giving thanks for Stéfan's birthday. Mia came running into the room, walked right up to Stéfan and hugged him tightly. She was very happy to see him and she congratulated him. Stéfan's cheeks dimpled deeply in delight.

On the morning of his birthday I told Stéfan about my vision. He was a little sad, but also happy about what I'd told him. I had taken the envelope with Mia's birthday money out of the safe and split it evenly. Stéfan could get his share, a gift from Mia. Morné would get his share later.

It was a distressing but special moment, like so many of my experiences those days: a strange mixture of pain and happiness.

Forgiveness

Some days the pain was replaced by feelings of guilt. Shortly before the summer of 2013, I experienced such a flurry of guilt. All my prayers revolved around forgiveness. Forgiveness from God, and forgiveness from Mia for not buckling her seatbelt that day. I stopped praying and realised my thoughts only revolved around her life that was.

That *was*, because I'd messed it up. I had not taken good care of my gift from God. There were many days that these kinds of emotions tossed me around like washing in a tumble dryer. Until, one morning during prayer, I got up from my knees and went to stand in front of the mirror. I looked at my reflection and said: "Mariska, I forgive you." I had realised that everyone had forgiven me, except me.

And then all the apologies came out. Sorry about the day at Tannie Charlene's when Mia had a wee-wee and I was impatient. Why did the events of that afternoon specifically torment me so much? I saw my tears in the mirror. For the first time. I also realised for the first time that I could begin to forgive myself. Even though I'd said it to myself numerous times before, that day was different. On the dressing table was a photograph of our family in a silver frame with a floral pattern, and in the photo Franché had his arm around me. I looked at the image of him and said out loud in front of the mirror that I also forgave him once again. Another, deeper layer of forgiveness.

And then I got tired of my teary face. I sat down next to my bed again and became still. And at that moment I felt Jesus lifting my chin and I clearly heard him say, "Do not have so little mercy on yourself. It is over. It is human. I am not angry. I forgive you."

As He said it, He was holding Mia in his arms. I heard her utter these momentous words: "Mom, I forgive you. Mom, I'm not angry at you. I like it here with Jesus. [She hugged Him more closely.] I'm waiting for you here, Mom."

Jesus held me against Him and I felt a small arm curl around my neck; Mia was hugging me too.

Thank you, Jesus. Amen.

For days after the forgiveness in front of the mirror I felt light, almost as if I were floating, until one morning in November when I had to do something at Mia's pre-primary school, Bambi. When I walked into the building, I saw posters for the Dance Mouse end-of-year event, and they were like a hit to the gut.

Of course, it was that time of year, a time for closing and saying goodbye. I'd been saying goodbye to everything since March. Mia was not going to be in the school concert at the end of the year. Why did it only occur to me then? The thought hit me like a bucket of cold water. I remembered the day in my kitchen when Mia snapped her fingers and gave a few dance steps while counting, "one, two, one, two," to stay in rhythm. I remembered how shy she'd been when she realised I'd been watching her. Flashbacks just kept hurting terribly, even after moments of forgiveness, like mine in front of the mirror.

My quiet time in my room rewarded me again later that day. In the usual place, I saw her once more: Mia came running towards me and pulled me by the arm so I'd go with her. She led me to a bench in the garden under large trees with big green leaves. At first I was alone, but them Jesus came to sit next to me. I saw my Mia organising friends to make sure everyone was standing in the correct place. They were putting on a concert for me. The little dancers' smiles never left their bright faces.

It was clear from an early age that Mia had a natural rhythm. Dear Tannie Alice who taught Kindermusik classes in Bloemfontein told us when my Mia was still little that she could dance. Now, my baby was dancing with Jesus. I don't know how these things work, but time and again Jesus fetched me from the darkest holes. He consoled me when it felt as if the pain had reached saturation point. He is just so incredibly faithful!

Light

Mourning has its place but also its limits.
– Joan Didion, *The Year of Magical Thinking*

New memories

My husband and our sons and I had spontaneously started doing fun things together again. For a long time I'd avoided creating new memories without Mia, but sometime during the three years after March 2013 I realised it was time for new memories, reminiscences that didn't include Mia.

During those three years, for weeks on end I had to consciously choose to get out of bed. There were days when I didn't want to live any more. There were days when I was angry with God, and there were days when all I wanted to do was to sit in His presence and weep.

Through it all, I was certain of one thing: God was never far from me. His daughter's pain broke His heart. I know that now. I also know that it was often a choice that I needed to make to go to Him for comfort. When I moved away from Him, I had to choose to go back. He was always there, waiting for me.

God knew exactly what I as a mother wanted to see in my darkest hours after Mia's death. I thank Him for every heavenly vision that He blessed me with. The reassurance I got that my little girl was living with Jesus, that she was happy and that I would one day hold her again was the consolation I needed, and still need. I give God all the glory for that.

The anguish abates over time, but it's certainly not a case of waiting for 365 days and, voilà, the pain is gone. Years later, I realised that a part of me would always pine for her—that was just a reality for everyone in our broken family. It's as if sorrow could find you and confront you. Sometimes it came out of the blue, and at other times I recognised the pattern of sorrow starting to build up inside me. Like a river in spate, there is no stopping it. You know the flood is on the way, and you know the damage it can cause.

There was a strange kind of comfort in this unpredictable pattern, perhaps because I knew the flood damage would always be repaired.

I want to state it clearly here that I did not figure out the grieving process and the experience of loss—by no means. I am, however, laughing again. And I believe this is the grace and hope we have in the comfort of our Heavenly Father.

In my opinion, there is no 10-step plan for getting over the death of a child. The day-to-day plan is a more appropriate description. Some days are difficult; others seem impossible; and every now and then you have a day that you get through and afterwards you think, today was not that bad. Just like the daily portion of manna that the Israelites received from God was good for one day, so was God's daily comfort to me. On Tuesday I would get through the day thanks to a plant bearing a new pink flower, but on Wednesday that symbol of hope would wither as I walk into a shop and see only blonde-haired girls. I'd need fresh manna again. Some days there was none. Some days the heavenly visions had to rescue me from the deepest valley. Other days having a cup of coffee with a good friend was enough.

It is an unpredictable journey.

You learn many lessons on this journey. The cliché that life is precious is surely the greatest of them all. Every moment of every day is an opportunity to make something beautiful of it. Do not wait until adversity strikes; live proactively and create memories, because that's all we get to keep of each other.

A potty chair becomes a flower pot

Mia's garden on our balcony was conceived in January 2014. I saw it as a kind of memory corner. The garden started out with a few big pots with plants that bear pink flowers. I placed things like a plastic crown and a high-heeled shoe without a mate among the flowers. Decorative butterflies that had been part of the flower arrangements at her memorial service also found a place in the garden, as did the big pink letters spelling "MIA" that we had on the sweets table at the service. Her wooden potty chair became a flower pot that occupied a place of honour in Mia's garden.

Another of Mia's things that were recycled was her tricycle with the white basket, which now has pride of place at our back door, with a bright-pink pelargonium planted in the basket. It started to bloom in February 2014 and has basically had flowers ever since. By March 2014, a year after that awful March of the accident, our balcony garden was a profusion of pink flowers such as impatiens and fuchsias.

The different kinds of pink flowers were symbolic of all the shades of longing in our home.

The pink memorials for Mia were attempts to alleviate the pain and, on reflection, an effort to make sure we didn't forget her. Was this the right and the best thing to do for every one of us? I don't know. In my opinion, there is no generic set of dos and don'ts to navigate the path of pain. Everything I set out to do was prompted by what my heart told me to do. Some of the efforts failed and left me with a paralysing feeling of despair, but others were and still are a source of hope.

On 27 March 2014 we commemorated that heart-breaking day in March 2013. Together, we lit a pink sky lantern near our house and let it float up into the sky. The first year without her was over.

I only just survived most of the firsts, but a few of them caught me off my guard, like the birthday party of a friend's daughter, or finding myself in the children's section in Woolworths looking to buy a gift for someone, or even just buying strawberries at the supermarket. The list of firsts was mercifully getting shorter. By April 2014, we knew it was time to start making other lists: to create new memories with our two sons. It was difficult to start planning a special holiday with them but without Mia. Keeping my head above water during this time was only possible thanks to the simple art of crochet, which became my saving grace.

While I was crocheting a blanket for Mia, hours would go by that I didn't say a word. I crocheted when the house got too quiet, or if I was looking for something to keep my hands busy, despite the weariness that was my constant companion. On weekends, especially, when the week's noise had faded, I crocheted.

I made the blanket in Mia's favourite colours, and crocheted special figures that reminded me of her on top of the bright-pink squares. She used to ask me if I would make her a blanket. Now I'd made one.

Mia got a mourning blanket.

Making memories without Mia

For the first 14 months after Mia's death, it was as if we each kept the little energy we had left for ourselves. We had nothing in reserve to share it with others, let alone embark on new projects. The Robberts family used to be good at projects, plans and adventures.

At some point after March 2014, Mia's two amazing brothers were the motivation for Project Overseas Holiday. An important stopover would be my brother's home in Switzerland, and then we would go to Italy (mainly to satisfy my obsession with that country), and then we'd take the boys to Disneyland Paris. With the planning for the holiday and the boys' jam-packed extracurricular programme of piano and tennis lessons, physio appointments and chess tournaments, I sometimes wanted to yell: Wait! Stop! Mia isn't here. How can we just go on like this? Until I realised we had no option but to go on.

When winter arrived in Bloemfontein—a time of year I would always wish away, especially during the previous winter, when it was not just the cold that cut me to the bone—our bags were packed for Europe, where it was summer.

Our holiday kicked off in a very hot Rome. There were many moments of cheerful laughter, gelato in hand, broken hearts well disguised in foreign parts. There, too, the sunset was once so pink that the pain rose to the surface. From the Ponte Vecchio, the Old Bridge, in Florence, the memories of Mia were painfully beautiful. We also visited our friend Thea, with whom we'd been supposed to have lunch in Stellenbosch on the day of the accident. She was spending the European summer at her cottage in the mountains in Northern Italy, so this was where we met again, on the other side of the world, in the shadow of a mountain. The same Thea who waited for us at the Boland hospital that fateful day. Together with Thea, we cried about that day again.

In Venice we were spoiled one day with a pink sunset over the canals, and in Zürich my brother was a hero to our two sons. It was the first time after Mia's memorial that we'd seen each other again. And it was precious. As a family we could even laugh again at the jokes he was so fond of telling, especially at the most unexpected moments.

Our last stop was Paris, France. At Notre-Dame cathedral we lit a candle for Mia, and there, among thousands of camera-wielding tourists, the great longing hit me again. I felt God's nearness intensely as I walked down an aisle, wiping away the tears, and sat down in a pew. I know that churches like this one and many other "tourist churches"

in Europe are more akin to museums or sights than the churches we know in South Africa, but even there Jesus was waiting for me. The "museum" was filled with His holiness.

Taking family photos at the Eiffel Tower with its thousands of twinkling lights in the evening was a painful experience for me, but I could see that the boys were awe-struck. At Disneyland Paris we all fervently missed Mia. Everything made us think of her. The four of us, united in longing, did all the fun rides together. We had so much fun that we laughed ourselves silly. Looking at the photos we took that day, they were the first ones in which our smiles were genuine. Was it the mutual recognition of our longing and the subsequent agreement to have fun despite it? I don't know, but what I do know is that the experience was etched in everyone's memory. Maybe it was even a turning point for us as a family.

As 2014 drew to a close, the plum tree we'd planted for Mia bloomed in a burst of tiny pink-and-white blossoms.

In November, with Franché's birthday coming up, I realised there was another first we'd have to work through. We'd made a habit of having family portraits taken by a professional photographer, and the time had come to have new photos taken. Our first photo shoot without Mia. During the previous two years I'd learnt that if you didn't confront these firsts head-on, they tended to stalk you like a thief in the night and kept daunting you. The more you tried to avoid them and the more you tried to forget about them, the less you succeeded in doing so. Before you knew it, you were spending all your time avoiding that which you feared.

I'd seen a photo at an exhibition long ago that I'd wanted to replicate in a family portrait, but I'd never got around to it. I phoned a photographer, the mother of a child that went to the same school as the boys, and I made an appointment. I had tears in my eyes by the time I ended the call.

The photo idea that I'd had in my head for all these years was only fitted in towards the end of the shoot. As is the case with such shoots, the photographer snapped away. She had us move closer together and further apart, and rearranged us for the perfect composition. When we got the first unedited photos a week later, I noticed that in my "dream photo" there was an open space between the two boys—a space that doesn't belong in a professional photo. In the edited photos, the four of us lay neatly and snugly against each other. To me, the "wrong" photo with the space between the boys was just right. That was Mia's spot. Somewhere in an album from 2012 there was a photo of Mia lying on her stomach, laughing—the perfect inset. And that's how my dream photo of us as a family became a reality. This portrait with the "gap" now has pride of place above our bed.

The December school holiday arrived—a second one without Mia. Our first stopover was at Ilzette and Richard's in Somerset West. The last time we'd seen them was shortly after the accident, nearly two years before. Then we went back to the place where Mia had been taken from us. Our goal on that hot December day was to plant a tree for her, a Cape chestnut. This tree with its pink flowers was the first pink memorial for Mia in the Cape. It hurt to be confronted with the place we associated with so much pain, but it was another first we could tick off.

Finally, we went to Franché's cousin in Jongensfontein, where there was another Mia in the household. This Mia has dark hair and olive skin, and differs only a few months in age from our blonde-haired Mia. This Mia also has a little sister, Ne'tjie. That December, my two sons played with their second cousins as if they were the last two girls on earth.

At Jongensfontein, nearly two years after Mia's death, I realised for the first time how much they missed the little sister they'd lost.

The hurt lessened
The year 2015 started on a good note. There were still frequent pink sunsets wherever we went. I started to call them my "pink letters". In January and February, we spent a few weekends with good friends, Anita and Johan, at Newbury Dam near Ladybrand. Time and again, the pink brush strokes on the dam's flat, calm water comforted me.

During the second 27 March that we had to get through, we were with them on their Bushveld[1] farm near Mookgophong(Naboom-

---

1. A sub-tropical woodland ecoregion of Southern Africa.

spruit). There, too, the veld[2] turned pink in the evenings. Mia's both-ers and our friends' children, actually everyone on the farm, could release a pink balloon for Mia. Inside the balloons each one could place a letter they'd written to her. I later heard that most of the letters were about how much they missed her and looked forward to seeing her again one day.

In the Bushveld, too, we were consoled.

A week after this anniversary in the north of the country, we were in Lambert's Bay on the West Coast. There, too, consolation was always near at hand. It became clearer to me: God's comfort followed me wherever I went. It was my choice whether I wanted to notice it or not, and for me that was vital.

The pink consolation became such a part of our lives that people who were close to us began to experience it with us. That's how it became a habit for our friends and their friends, wherever they were in the world, to send us photos of beautiful pink sunsets. If you read this book and God moves you to send us a photo of a pink sunset, feel free to do so: my email address is mariska.robberts@gmail.com. Every photo gives me the reassurance that my little pink girl's sudden depar-ture from earth has touched many lives. Every sunset is a consolation that Mia is with God, but for many others it may be a reminder of the greatness of the Creator. Mia highlighted this greatness for us in pink.

During the first two years after Mia's death, the visual highlight was seeing these sunsets. The other highlight was the company of good friends and family. It is entirely normal to be inundated with visitors after an accident like ours, but as time goes by, most people get on

---

2. Veld, also spelled veldt, is a type of wide open rural landscape in Southern Africa.

with their lives and the visitors get fewer and fewer. Yet some friends and family were always there for us. Since I've been on the receiving end of empathy, I've realised the importance of treating the wounded as normally as possible. I also know it's anything but easy because there are so many awkward silences and unpredictable crying fits when you spend time with wounded people. Not to mention the constant treading on eggshells to avoid saying something that would make the pain flare up.

Once we could lift our heads again, ordinary social interaction with people who treated us as if we were still the same Robberts family as before meant the most to me. It was after one such ordinary visit with friends that I was able to gather the courage to "tackle" Mia's room. I first took a picture of her cluttered wardrobe and the toys that were still lying just as she'd left them. I wanted to remember her room that way. And then I started to sort things out. Every object in that room was worth its weight in gold, from the rolled-up hair elastic (with strands of her hair still caught in it) and the useless hair slide to her newest doll with the golden locks. I cried an awful lot, because I knew it was part of the reality I didn't want to accept and with which I didn't want to make peace. In that room, one by one, things started to fall into place.

As I was sorting out and packing up Mia's things, I thought again of how much I wanted to create something meaningful out of my suffering. Before the winter of 2015, I realised I'd better give away some of her clothes before they'd be too small for Nina, a friend's daughter who was younger than Mia. I chose the most beautiful things for Nina: vests from 2013 for the winter of 2015, vests with the price tags still attached, vests without price inflation but with very high pain inflation.

I kept the rest of her clothes to take with us on our winter holiday to Mozambique. The immense poverty we'd seen on our previous visit had touched me deeply—as well as the tremendous gratitude of the people for anything you gave them. I hoped that Mia's old clothes, which were as precious as gold to me, would also brighten other people's lives. My sentiment and their poverty transcended all differences: the broad smiles with which each piece of clothing was received were a solace.

It made me feel good to give away Mia's clothes and toys, but there were a few of her things that I couldn't let go. For these, I had a memory box made out of wood (painted pink, of course). I placed a handful of Mia's most precious knick-knacks in it. I thought that if forgetting came with healing, I could always turn to this box.

The pain did ease, and now and then there was even a little forgetting, but the longing grew more and more intense. On days when the longing was fierce, I sometimes watched home videos of her to remind me what her voice had sounded like. Photo albums had to help me remember details of her short life.

By December 2015, we were ready to bury her ashes, still in the wooden urn, at Bambi Pre-Primary. At the time of her death, this school was her second-most favourite place in the world. Next to the spot where we buried the urn we planted a pride of India. This tree is located next to the school's boundary fence, on the corner of Bompart and General Hertzog streets, so that we could see her tree whenever we drove past—especially in summer when it flaunts its beautiful pink flowers for all the world to see.

The 'Candy Stripe' rose that we'd planted at the school soon after Mia's memorial service had a few magnificent flowers when we were there to bury the urn with her ashes. Traces of Mia can be found everywhere on the grounds of the pre-primary school: in the leaves and flowers of the pride of India, among the striped petals of the rosebush, and on the school's well-known mosaic alumni wall. I had to write her name on the wall next to the other names of the class of 2013, because she was already gone by then.

As we drove away after the ceremony at Bambi, four snow-white doves settled on the strip between the traffic lanes. These doves reminded me of the angels that God sent to walk with the four of us. Our angels are always with us, wherever we go. We just don't always notice them...until the pain of being in the world without a loved one opens your eyes, searching for signs of hope.

Healing through art

In 2016 I started to take art classes. I'm one of those people who'd always wanted to be artistic but could barely draw a stickman. The creative ideas in my head was where the art stopped. Or so I'd thought.

When a long-time friend invited me, I accompanied her to her art class. My first attempt at wielding a paintbrush will forever remain a secret to the world—for the simple reason that it was lousy. Yet the failed attempt had awakened something in me, and I went back to the class. I learnt a whole lot and made steady progress. The paintings in which I incorporated different elements of my Mia journey brought a different kind of healing, something I can confidently call peace. When I look at my paintings, I really don't know how I managed to make them. Each one is precious to me, because it's something I created with my own two hands, something I'd believed for 40 years I didn't have the skill to do. Every painting was informed by a specific Bible passage, which became more real with each stroke of the paintbrush.

With hearts more whole than the previous December holiday, we returned to Jongensfontein in December 2016. Dark-haired Mia and her sister Ne'tjie had obviously grown bigger and were not as shy as before. Again, my boys did not miss a chance to join then in playing on the beach, watching TV or eating ice cream. Between Christmas—which had not really become any easier—and my birthday on 28 December, the longing was again intense. Dark-haired Mia must have sensed it, because on the morning of the 28th she unexpectedly came to sit on my lap and asked whether I'd watch a story on TV with her. After a while her sister joined her. And there I was, on my birthday, with two little girls on my lap. Despite my sore heart, I experienced the same feeling of being spoiled as with a pink sunset and my visits to the throne room.

My birthday presents increased. Later that day, we went to Mossel Bay with friends and family, and there, at a restaurant on the beach, I ran into a new friend from Bloemfontein "by chance". My friendship with Liezl had begun the day she gave me the pink tulips, the tulips that confirmed my first heavenly encounter with Mia. Liezl, the messenger. Our friendship was still young, so I was surprised to discover we shared a birthday. On the very day that we ran into each other by chance at a restaurant in Mossel Bay. Jesus had truly chosen his messenger personally!

The year 2016 ended on a good note. I should have known it would have a good ending, because it had been predicted in August already. It was still winter when I travelled to the Cape with a few friends to support my son Stéfan, who was there for a choir competition. The day after the competition in Stellenbosch, I revisited that sad place on Bottelary Road with two friends, Annemarie and Elna, with whom we were staying in Melkbosstrand. It had been three-and-a-half years. I'd bought a bunch of pink proteas at a market to place next to the cross we'd planted for Mia. The small cross was hidden in the long grass next to the busy road. The rainfall must have been good that winter, because the place I associated with only sorrow was covered with bright-white arum lilies as far as the eye could see. The showy flowers of this plant—which is not actually a lily nor an arum—are a popular choice for bridal bouquets.

God's bride, I said to myself, because that afternoon among the arum lilies I thought, could a place imbued with so much sadness be this beautiful? Was it possible? Or was the wall of my heart slowly but surely growing a new layer?

Something to lift our spirits

In 2017, our lives started to take on a new focus. A whole other dimension of hope emerged for us as a family.

Stéfan was in Grade 7 at the time and Morné in Grade 5. High school beckoned for Stéfan.

It was alarming to realise how fast the years had flown by. Before we knew it, the little boys who'd had to walk a difficult path of healing with us had grown up.

Stéfan and Morné both suffer from a muscle condition that limits mobility. They find it difficult, for example, to climb stairs. The time that schools allow learners to walk from one classroom to the next between periods is often not long enough for them. But their friends at school spontaneously started to carry their bags so they could move without that extra weight and try to arrive in time for the next class.

We'd chosen to send the boys to a mainstream primary school. They were certainly not the fastest in the school, but they were very happy and they coped well. They had close friends and good teachers, and they had memories of playing mini rugby when they were younger, Voortrekker[3] camps and choir tours. In the lower grades they even had the opportunity now and then to play hockey.

Stéfan has beautiful memories of friends carrying him on their back or teachers helping him onto the tour bus. There are also precious memories of friends helping them get up a steep river bank or to the top of a Free State koppie[4].

---

3. An Afrikaner youth organisation, founded in South Africa in 1931.

4. A small hill in a generally flat area.

In short, everyone was fond of Stéfan and Morné, not only because of the grace with which they accepted their limitation, but also—and especially—because of their tenacity. What they lack physically, they make up for in terms of spirit.

I still learn from them about endurance and perseverance. They fall often, literally, but they always get up. There are no more rugby or hockey games on their schedule because the competition among schools has become too fierce, but you'll see them standing next to the field.

When Stéfan and Morné reached their teens, their afternoons became filled with chess and piano lessons, and they threw themselves into drama and swimming. Without their sister but not without passion—that's how I tend to think of my two sons. In fact, that is all Franché and I ever wanted: children who are as passionate about life as we are. That decision had been made before Mia's death, and now it was all the more necessary to remind ourselves of it.

The boys' primary school days, happy ones to a large extent, were coming to an end. A new challenge lay ahead of us: which high school would be the right one for them? Would we have to cut ties with long-time friends for the sake of greater mobility for them? The school to which most of Stéfan's friends planned to go wasn't Stéfan-friendly. Although this high school had sent him an invitation letter based on his music talent to continue his schooling and music studies there in 2018, the school layout was not suitable for him. The primary school where he was had only two storeys, but the high school had three storeys and the pace was much faster. How would Stéfan keep up with it?

The year 2017 was only two months young when I started to get quotes to have a lift installed at the high school. I got the necessary documentation together and wrote a letter to the Department of Basic

113

Education to ask for permission to have a lift installed at the school at our own expense. I knew that if I were to ask them for the funds it would never happen. I still had no idea where the money would come from, but I lived in hope!

Getting approval from, among others, the school board and the department was an elaborate, drawn-out process. Plans had to be drawn up and submitted to the municipality. This, too, took months.

The estimated cost for the lift and the shaft was about R438 000. I remember how I made it sound doable by saying it would only take 400 people each giving about R1 000 each. I had no idea how I would raise the money, but I was determined to make this dream come true for my sons.

I started the project by designing a digital brochure on my computer with photos of Stéfan and Morné, information about their muscle condition, and a request for help in making the boys' dream to go to this school a reality—and hopefully also for many other boys and girls in the future. We sent it via WhatsApp to everyone we knew and everyone they knew. The first R1 000 was deposited in our account in April. As time passed, donations trickled in from friends and acquaintances. I got a call from the mother of Morné's best friend at school, Gretha, who was the organiser of a hockey tournament at the school. She suggested linking it up with the Robberts Support Fund, as we'd since named the fund. During the two-day tournament we could run a tuck shop selling food, cool drinks and coffee. Thanks to sponsorships, the help of friends, men wielding braaitongs[5] and women with nimble hands, we raised thousands of Rands over the two days.

---

5. Braai is South Africa's barbecue.

Thus one door after the other began to open. We were blown away by the generosity and kindness of the people of Bloemfontein. Corette, who worked for Franché, kindly organised an evening function involving an auction, which was attended by more than 250 guests. Stéfan and Morné even bravely performed a piano piece each for the audience. The Robberts hope meter rose sharply. The fund was growing, and the goal of raising R438 000 started to seem within reach.

The year was halfway gone and we had passed the halfway mark to our dream when Stéfan and I went to record a video of him at the front steps of his prospective high school. While he climbed the steps, he asked people to help him realise his dream of having a lift installed at this school. We posted the video on Facebook, and it was soon shared on WhatsApp and spread further afield. I got a shock when I had a look one day and saw how many times it had been watched and shared. Is that what "going viral" means? I wondered.

I really had no words to describe God's goodwill with the lift project. People I'd never met before, from all over the country and even from beyond South Africa's border, contacted me and donated money. And these were difficult economic times. People just gave; they gave unconditionally. There were large donations from businesses, huge payments made anonymously, and R25 from a brother of one of Morné's friends. He'd taken the R25 from his piggy bank and gave it to me when we visited them on their farm near Bethulie one weekend.

Quite a few organisations held fundraisers on their own initiative and donated the proceeds to us, even though we hadn't asked for it. We also received a generous gift of a promotional video that told our story, professionally produced by the parents of a girl in Morné's class. We could use the video at all the fundraising events, and later also posted it on social media to raise awareness of the lift project.

The local newspapers supported us by placing free articles, and a local community radio station gave us airtime to tell our story.

To cut a long story short, *everyone* helped.

All the contractors, including the architect, the structural engineer and the building contractor, did their part of the work for free. It was hope in action! The two schools involved—the boys' primary school and high school of choice—also helped wherever they could.

There was an evening of praise and worship at a local congregation with the band Onbeskaamd to raise the last of the money we needed. The band performed for free, the auditorium was made available free of charge, and the Lord's Name was praised as the last bit of money for the lift project came in.

An entire community had joined hands to make it possible for Morné and Stéfan to go to the high school of their choice. Within seven months! We were amazed.

Beyond all expectations, the municipality approved the plans for the lift by September 2017; there were only four months left before Stéfan was to start high school. Some parts for the lift were delayed at customs, but despite that the installation could start on 2 January 2018. The final approval was completed a few days before the start of the school year. Everything had worked out perfectly, and my child could face his first day of high school with self-confidence –with a lift to give it a boost.

At the start of this project I looked for a Bible verse to hold on to, and the one I found was 1 John 4:4. I had the promise in this verse printed on thank-you cards and fridge magnets, and the words figure in big letters in the lift: "The Lord is greater than the giants we face."

And this has been proven true, over and over.

Hope springs eternal

Hope has always been a part of my path of life, regardless of the challenges that have come my way over the years. Before our Robberts family lost one member, and after that.

In 2010, we started to hope for a fourth child. Paging through my dairies, I see that I wrote it down in October 2010, just after we'd added a fourth bedroom to our house. More than a year later I wrote in my diary, during a holiday in Ballito, that God had told me through His Word that we would have another baby.

In 2012, the dream of a fourth child became a desire. I started to take medication to improve our chances of getting pregnant—it's human nature to get impatient when things are not going according to your plan.

While writing this chapter about hope, I found something in my diary that I'd jotted down in 2012. It was a question Mia had asked: "Mommy, when is our baby sister coming?"

I'd wanted with all my heart to give Mia an answer to her question, but I couldn't. Not then. In the end I would never answer her question, at least not in the way that people on earth give answers.

The burning desire for another baby regularly opened up an entire spectrum of emotions, from disappointment and frustration to discouragement and sometimes anger. Only when I myself started out on this path of struggling to get pregnant did I realise how difficult it was. It is a path that numerous women walk in silence every day. You live in a two-week cycle of ovulation to menstruation, month after month.

During this time, the pages of my diary were filled with Bible verses speaking of hope. One of my anchor verses was John 11:40 (NLT), which I highlighted in my diary:

Jesus responded, "Didn't I tell you that you would see God's glory if you believe?"

Then, 27 March 2013 dawned.

The wish for another busy little one wasn't quelled by the pain that followed that dark day. We even went to a fertility clinic five months later on the recommendation of my gynaecologist.

Franché and I were both on the wrong side of 30, so it was a race against time for us. After a number of failed intrauterine insemination procedures, the disappointment became too much for us. At the beginning of 2014, I underwent two in-vitro fertilisation cycles. Success kept eluding us. I cried harder each time, until I realised one day that I might be wanting this baby too much. It had subconsciously become more than a desire. It was now an obsession. I admitted this to my Heavenly Father.

After much wrestling with myself I had to admit that it was clearly not the right time and that God didn't want to give us a child just then. Thinking back now, I realise the Lord knew that there were other things we needed to concentrate on at the time. Only later did it also dawn on me that it wasn't only about *my* readiness and *my* desire, but also about my sons' and my husband's. They, too, had to be ready for a new addition to our family.

Was I truly ready for it?
In May 2014, a very good friend Anneléne (or 'Lien as Mia named her), took me to a man by the name of Jan who would pray with me and make prophesies. This visit came after I'd had a particularly difficult week. Jan told me that the Lord saw that I was very insecure and that my heart was overflowing with questions without answers. Like so many others had in recent months, Jan affirmed that I would

have a ministry one day. He also told me of a vision he had of me wearing a white dress walking through a green field with beautiful pink flowers. In the vision I danced and rejoiced. He then asked me whether I liked the colour pink. Jan knew nothing of the roll that pink played in my grieving process. It was, after all, the first time we'd met.

Jan told me that my marriage would be rebuilt. He also prophesied that we would wake up one morning and be pregnant—without any treatment or medication. He even saw the gender of this promised baby and added that he knew we wanted a baby girl. He also talked to me about our sons' challenges, and said God wanted us to trust that He was in control.

The message was clear: a new season would dawn for us.

When Jan prayed for me, I felt the gentle breeze of the Holy Spirit against my skin.

After our restorative family holiday in Europe, I discovered that I was pregnant. The news was like a shiny dewdrop hanging on the tip of a green leaf early in the morning after a long, dark night.

The joy was short-lived, however, because at a follow-up visit to the doctor she told us she couldn't detect a heartbeat. She gave us some more time, and shared our hope in a miracle.

On the day before our next doctor's visit, I prayed to my Heavenly Father and beseeched Him to let our baby live. I felt myself giving the baby to Jesus and saw how she started to glow and fidget in His hands. I wasn't sure what this vision meant: would there be a miracle, or was the baby already living with Him?

The next day at the doctor's consulting room I had to find out that it meant the latter. More loss. More pain.

I cried at my Father's feet and felt in my heart that my baby had been a girl. I prayed and asked my Father to give her a name.

I named her Anya Tahila. Here's why:

Anya is derived from Hannah, which has its roots in the Hebrew for "God's grace", "God's gift of grace" or "an answered prayer". A second interpretation of this name is of Irish origin and means "brilliance, radiance and splendour".

The Hebrew root of the name Tahila means "heavenly dew", "dew from God" or "richly blessed". A second meaning comes from the Aramaic for "little girl" or "lamb."

While I prayed and wept at my Father's feet, He reminded me of a previous miscarriage. My Father showed me that maybe it was time to also name that baby. I'd never had a spiritual experience about that miscarriage before. As I spent time in God's presence, the image of a dirty little boy with curly blond hair came to me, and in my ear I heard the name Christoff.

I wasn't immediately convinced. That wasn't the name I'd had in mind, I thought to myself. But then I clearly heard the words, "His name is Christoff, because "he is of Christ."

That day, for the first time, I saw Mia with her little sister Anya, wrapped in a blanket, and the blond boy standing next to her. There was a strong focus on the unity between these three children in heaven and our family here on earth. A supernatural peace washed over me during this experience. They were together, and they were waiting for us. I have treasures in heaven too, and we don't always realise how close it actually is to us—so close I could feel it.

After this heavenly encounter I had a look in my diaries to see how old this little boy would have been. He would have been about two. Everything I'd seen of this little boy in heaven was typical of a two-year-old.

In January 2015, I read the following paragraph in my Joyce Meyer Bible:

I have discovered that the secret to being content is to ask God for what I want and to rest in the knowledge that if it is right, He will bring it to pass at the right time. If it is not right, He will do something much better than what I asked for.

This was balm to my heart, which still wouldn't let go of the longing for another baby. But, in all honesty, this "resting" was easier said than done. To place my burden at my Father's feet, and to leave it there...or to return the burden over and over after I'd fetched it from Him again... In this way, I took my burden back to His feet many times.

The desire remains

The months became years, and the desire for another child remained in my heart. I even asked the Lord to remove this desire from my heart because at times it was too painful to carry.

Sometimes I relaxed about wanting another baby, but I have to confess that the desire never ever went away. As my friends grew older with me and began to conclude their child-bearing phase, I started to wonder whether it wasn't time for me, too, to close this book.

One by one, my friends got rid of their baby stuff. I couldn't do it.

In February 2016, Franché and I attended a weekend of praise and worship with Mervis van der Merwe. On the Friday evening I experienced sitting at Jesus' feet. Mia was lying on her stomach in front of Him, propped up on her elbows and watching me while I praised Him.

Soon after this wonderful experience Mervis began to talk about how we should focus on God's love for us and not only on our love for Him. I felt Jesus stroking my hair and my head resting against his chest. Later, we were in the garden and I was lying with my head on

His lap. Mia walked up to us and came to lie in my arms, tightly against my body. We enjoyed the moment of Jesus' embrace. It was one of the most precious moments I ever experienced of God's nearness. It was almost tangible.

The next day's message was that God doesn't have to do anything for us. He is God of the universe. He doesn't owe us anything, and we actually don't deserve anything. But, out of His treasure house of love, God nevertheless provides for us in abundance. Mervis also referred to God's greatest sacrifice, to offer His Son to take our place on the cross. We should thank Him a lot more than we do.

At some point during the praise sessions I felt God taking my hand and guiding me to get up from my kneeling position on the floor. Just like Jesus had done it in the past, God pulled me onto his lap...

I was aware of the light radiating from Him—His full glory. Everything around me was very bright. The next moment, I was dancing before His throne. I experienced God's approval and His love like never before.

In the flesh I would have been too self-conscious to dance like that, but before my great Father I danced freely and with abandon. I saw Mia giggling behind her hands as she watched me dancing before the Father. At that moment I clearly felt His approval. It helped me to let go of my last bit of shyness. I looked my Father in the eye and prayed: "Lord God, I ask once more, will I get pregnant again? You know that it has been our hearts' desire since 2012."

I clearly saw the Father nodding His head. In his eyes I saw that He was saying yes. For the first time in a long while, I got an answer to this question.

I felt a little overwhelmed and wondered whether it could be true. Had I understood Him correctly?

I looked up at God again and asked if I'd heard Him correctly. That's when it was confirmed, because Jesus nodded His head too.

There was no doubt: I would have another child and, like in Hannah's life, it would become a part of my testimony, a testimony of the Father's wondrous glory.

My experience didn't stop there. I saw Mia getting excited and laughing behind her hands, and telling her friends what was lying ahead for us.

More than one person had prophesied another child without knowing of the desire in our hearts, but as the years passed my faith in this dream had started to fade away. Until that evening's praise session where Mervis repeatedly said that God didn't have to be there and that God didn't have to do anything for us. Yet He was with us and He worked miracles for us.

My heart was filled to the brim with hope. I was convinced another baby would come into our lives, and it would be a miracle of God that would proclaim His glory. My age wouldn't matter.

One last time

Later that year we decided on one last fertility treatment. I didn't know it then, but as I started to write this chapter early in 2019 I realised it was a desperate decision made in the flesh. By that time it had been nearly six months since my experience at the praise evening, and still there was no sign of a pregnancy.

It was a very difficult place to be—where you believe you'd received a promise of something, but months and years have gone by and you've seen nothing of that promise come true. As your despair increases, you start to make human decisions.

The year was not over yet when I saved the number of one of the best fertility clinics in Johannesburg on my phone. We wanted to give ourselves the best chance, medically speaking, to get pregnant. My brother in Switzerland made a contribution to pay the clinic's bill.

Shortly before this treatment would begin, I experienced God again.

I saw myself setting at a table laid for a banquet. The table was in a room that looked like a fairy-tale ballroom. Everything on the table was perfect; the only thing that was lacking was the food. I was trusting that the king, one of the guests, would bring the food. All I had to do was set the table. Every now and then I peered out of the window, looking for the king and the food. Finally I saw him approaching, with a velvet cloak draped over his shoulders.

I realised that the symbolism spoke of God's nearness, always, whether we act within His will or not. He is always beside us, no matter the beginning and the end.

It was almost a year after this experience that I realised I'd never written it down that there was no food at the banquet. I'd only written about the king I'd seen, the king that was on his way. It's quite ironic that it took me so long to realise that I wasn't acting within my King's will. I was just assuming that God would provide according to my timing; I could go ahead and set the table.

Due to my "advanced age" the clinic could retrieve only two eggs from me to send for tests. A few days later I got a call from the doctor. At the same time an email was sent to me to confirm what I was told: we could not go ahead with the implantation because they had detected serious abnormalities in both fertilised eggs. They'd be two boys who wouldn't be viable. Again we were broken.

Our last and best attempt had failed. I wondered if our path had come to a dead end.

I started to get rid of our baby stuff. God was there—also during these clear displays of my lack of faith.

How do you make peace with something when His Word has been spoken but the contrary is your reality? I was constantly trapped in an inner conflict. I reasoned myself into corners. And when I was stuck, I chose not to think any further...until the whole process would repeat itself.

At the end of 2016, I started to talk to a counsellor, Hanja Ziehl. Hanja is a remarkable woman who walks a genuine path with the Lord. She helped me a lot to work free the pain that was lodged in me and wouldn't budge, like wiggling loose a milk tooth. She is much more than a counsellor. She also has the gift of prophesy. Before I met her, I struggled to forgive someone. She helped me with that too, since my inability to forgive this person was responsible for a lot of damage in my life, especially in my marriage.

During one of our last sessions, at the beginning of 2017, she walked in and said to me, "Mariska, I prayed for you this morning, and the Lord impressed on me that you need to write a book about your journey after Mia's death. This book that you'll write will complete your healing. And then, and only then, will you become pregnant."

She told me I was standing in my own way and that I had to start writing.

In the next few months, with the encouragement of another special friend and sister in Jesus, Erika, I wrote down the first words. I really didn't know how to go about writing a book. Where do you begin?

In September 2017, I attended a service at a small church on the outskirts of Bloemfontein with Liezl, my tulip friend and sister in Jesus. This church has a great healing and prophesy ministry, and we'd felt the need to experience it that day. We really enjoyed the service, and afterwards the pastor started to call random worshippers to the front to pray for and minister to them. At the end of the ministry he walked down the aisle and pointed his finger at me. I half-turned my head to see who he was pointing at when he said, "You in the pink (yes, I wore pink that day too), please come forward." I got up and walked to the front.

He started to talk to me and told me he could see that I loved the Lord very much, and that I held on to Him with all my being through all the difficult times and losses in my life. He picked up a bottle of water and demonstrated how I was holding on to the Father, with a wobbly hand that sometimes threatened to slip. He went on to say that the Lord had shown him that he had to comfort me. He talked a little more about other things in my life and then concluded with the following: "When the Lord blesses you again, lady, do you know what I mean when I say He is going to bless you again?" I softly asked him whether it meant a baby, because my little girl was in heaven.

He nodded and said, "Don't look at your womb, lady; look at the Lord."

The pastor then prayed with me, and Liezl and I went home with excitement in our hearts.

The months passed. Colette, another God-given angel and friend in my life, agreed to help me write the book. She edited the text and found a golden thread to weave through all the words that flowed from me. The last pieces of the puzzle fell into place thanks to Colette's experience as a writer. And they fitted neatly. Despite our busy lives, there were miraculously hours left to weave the threads together into a narrative.

In 2018, after my annual visit to the gynaecologist, I found out I had a growth on my cervix, located in a place where it could not be removed without also having to perform a hysterectomy. It was a prospect that didn't bear thinking about, not after everything I'd been through over the past few years.

I knew I was on borrowed time. I'd been struggling with an iron deficiency for many years as a result of heavy menstrual flow each month. My doctor also suspected that the growth was rapidly becoming larger and more visible because of all the hormones associated with the fertility treatment. She said it could be part of the problem why I couldn't fall pregnant.

I walked out of her consulting room knowing that if I were to get pregnant, it would be a huge miracle.

As 2018 progressed, we wrote the last chapters of the book you're now holding in your hands.

On Monday, 21 January 2019, Colette sent me the first draft of the book by email. It was nearly a month after the date we'd hoped to complete the first draft. I was nevertheless incredibly excited that we had something to work with; finally there was something tangible on the table.

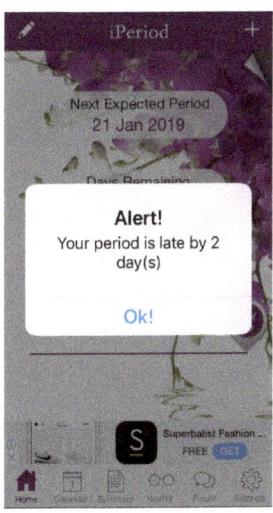

According to the app on my phone that I'd been using for a long time to monitor my cycle so I wouldn't be caught unawares by a heavy menstrual flow, 21 January 2019 was the day on which my period was supposed to start. But that didn't happen.

I gave it another two days because I thought it might just be taking a little longer that month. Two days later I decided to take the big step: I would go to buy a home pregnancy test kit and use it. I bought two different kits, threw them into my handbag and tried not to think about how many such test kits I'd bought in the past. And especially not about how many of them had landed in the bin with only one line in the result window—accompanied by enormous disappointment in my heart.

I returned home and quietly went to my room. Both tests were positive.

I was speechless. I phoned my aunt who is a medical doctor, and she sent me an application form for a blood test. Soon after I went to the pathology lab. I hesitantly put down the form on the counter. The woman behind it asked me about the bracelet I was wearing, the one with Mia's name engraved on it. I told her about Mia who was now in heaven. And she told me she also had a child in heaven.

The magical moments were not over yet. The nurse who drew my blood, I heard, also had children in heaven: two babies born prematurely, one of whom would have been a year old that day. Behind the sliding door of a cramped room, for a brief time, Tumi and I shared each other's deepest pain. Until that day we had been strangers to each other, strangers with the same pain and unanswered questions. I couldn't help telling her about my years of hoping for another baby. And, of course, about the book I was busy writing and the miracle that would transpire that day. I firmly believed it, even though my belief was still only based on a home test.

We both had tears in our eyes as I talked to her about the familiar pain and the great void that arises between God and his children as a result of such a loss. On that day, I could encourage her with words that were true for me: The Lord understands your pain and He understands your lack of faith in Him. Just know that it's not Him but the enemy who stole from you.

I signed my name on the labels for the blood-collection tubes, wiped away my tears and walked out. The woman behind the counter, unaware of what had happened between Tumi and me behind the closed sliding door, said to me: "Mrs Robberts, you coming in here today, there's a purpose to it."

The greater scope of the Father's plan with my ministry's very first baby steps was now becoming visible.

About an hour later the news was confirmed: I was pregnant. Two days later I received the first draft of the book.

At the insistence of my aunt, I went back for another blood test two days later. This time, the level of hCG hormone in my blood sample had more than doubled.

At eight weeks, we visited the gynaecologist for an ultrasound examination. In the dark room we saw the proof of life, and seconds later we heard the heartbeat. Franché and I were both overwhelmed by tears of joy and gratitude.

It was a very special moment for us, since I'd been very anxious in the few days before the ultrasound, especially because of the experience in 2014 when our baby didn't have a heartbeat. I prayed fervently, but the enemy did his best to bombard my mind with false ideas.

As if the day wasn't exceptional enough, later that morning, as I was sharing the joyous news with a few friends, "by chance" I saw a photo that my cousin Tanja had shared on Facebook with respect to her acting career. It was a photo of a jubilant woman in a white dress, in a field of pink cosmos flowers. It was the exact image Jan had described in his 2014 prophecy, which was later confirmed with a special prayer and prophecy by my friend Carla during an event one morning held for the helpers at our church's children's ministry. It was another confirmation of God's involvement in my journey of hope and his nearness to me.

One of my anchor Bible verses, which I've always marked with a highlighter in my diary, took on a new meaning for me:

So will My word be
Which goes out of My mouth;
It will not return to Me void (useless, without result);
Without accomplishing what I desire.,
And without succeeding in the matter for which I sent it.

– Isaiah 55:11

This verse left me speechless. For me, eight years later, the Word became flesh in my womb. Despite everything that had happened, I had kept my eyes fixed on the Lord.

Thank You, Heavenly Father. Amen.

Blue II

Samuel, will you lend Me your ear?
This is the voice of your Father here
If I speak the word and no one has the vision
Can I count on you, my sweet child, to listen?
Samuel, lend Me your ear.
There will be days you feel like flying
Then there'll be days you feel like crying
Never give up, never stop trying
Never believe my love is dying.
– From the song "Samuel" by Jason Upton

August, a month of wind and greatness

August, the eighth month. A month that we in the Free State associate with wind and the last spasms of winter. The landscape looks particularly dreary. But the origins of the word "august" convey a very different message; inherent in it are majesty, grandeur and hallowed things.

Here in the Southern Hemisphere in the central parts of South Africa, a summer-rainfall region, August is anything but majestic or grand.

Until...

But before I get to "until", I should start with "because".

Because of the new life growing inside me, I endured weeks of severe fatigue and nausea. During our 12-week prenatal visit the doctor told us about the latest screening tests. They're different to the tests I'd undergone during my pregnancy with Mia 10 years before. She said these newer tests were much more accurate in detecting any potential disorders, such as Down's syndrome.

Because of my advanced age—I'd turned 44 in 2019—these tests were important. A week later I visited the pathology lab for blood tests. And a day later the boys and I left for Stellenbosch, where they were to participate in a national swimming event. By the time we set out I hadn't received the results of the blood tests yet.

We were close to our destination when I got a call from my doctor, who sounded excited. The results of the tests were negative, which meant no abnormalities had been detected. She also told me that we were expecting a boy.

I was exceedingly grateful but stunned, too. A boy? I tried to make sense of it, because in my mind I was carrying a sister for Stéfan and Morné. In the flesh I had started "to pink". For me, "pink" had long since ceased to be an adjective; in recent years "to pink" had become a verb. To pink was to be excited about little girls and everything associated with them. I'd also swept up everyone close to me in this pink excitement.

Annemarie, my friend who was accompanying me to the Cape, teasingly said to me, "Aren't you also wondering if the doctor didn't have the wrong person's file in front of her when she called you?" We giggled about it, but my emotions were in turmoil and wouldn't settle down.

Soon after that we turned off the N1 highway, and I pointed out the turn-off to Bottelary Road to Annemarie—a road that to me would surely always be associated with pain.

I dropped Annemarie off at friends of hers, and the boys and I went to stay at close friends of ours who'd moved from Bloemfontein to the Cape a few months earlier. They were now living a stone's throw from

Mediclinic Stellenbosch, a place familiar to us for all the wrong and painful reasons.

During the next few days among the Boland mountains, we focused only on the swimming event. I made sure I knew when we had to be where and tried to keep the boys calm and motivated. Only later did I realise that a storm had started to pick up inside me.

On the second-last day of the event I had some time alone. Our friends were still at work and the boys were resting before their next swimming session. There was load shedding[1] again. For others an annoyance, destined for me. I had to force myself to stop and face the storm.

I became quiet in my room. I sat down at my Father's feet and gave my questions, my uncertainty and my arrogance to Him.

How many times have I had to do this? I end up in a mess by following my own head and convincing myself of things the way I thought would be best. And then I'd go to my Father in tears and ask Him to help me. Yet every time He'd meet me with open arms, with no reproach or anger, only with patience and the knowledge of a much larger picture than the one I could see.

That day I asked the Lord for a soft, penetrating rain in my heart that could wash away everything I had wrongly dished up for myself in recent weeks...that could change my certitudes so I'd be able to see the picture that God saw.

I cried until I had no tears left to get rid of all the emotions that had built up inside me. And I got up (again) with a heart filled with

---

1. An energy utility's method of reducing demand on the energy generation system by temporarily switching off the distribution of energy to certain geographical areas.

hope that what I had asked for would become my reality, even though I wasn't feeling it yet.

That afternoon I sent messages to a few close friends to tell them about the test results. This was Liezl's response:

I hope you don't mind me telling you that I knew it was a boy. I was praying about your baby one day while brushing my teeth, even before you'd gone for the heartbeat-ultrasound. I then got the impression that it was a boy. In my mind I immediately went to Hannah's story and saw how she had pleaded with the Lord for Samuel. I sensed that the Lord was sending you a Samuel. He will become a spokesman for God—for many nations! There will be nothing ordinary about this little boy. God needs you to raise him to live out his calling. I am so excited! He was called by his name to do something very special for God here on earth. And you were chosen.

Later, she sent me a second message:

See, I am doing a new thing! Now it springs up; do you not perceive it? I am making a way in the wilderness and streams in the wasteland.
– Isaiah 43:19 (NIV)

God's plan for what is next isn't about repackaging what He's already done. No, He is doing a new thing. So rather than looking for the "next", I want to encourage you to look for the new! Let God do a new thing in and through your life. He has awesome plans for you!
– Christine Caine

Suddenly, the lyrics of "The Garden Song" by the singer-songwriter Jason Upton from Wisconsin sounded like a prophesy:

I wanna build you a garden
In a dry and desert land
I'm gonna find a river there
I'm gonna find a river there
I have seen a garden grow
In a land filled with injustice
I have heard a mother's cry
For her child to live again
I have seen a withered soul
Fall like petals on the water
I have watched a flower grow
Slowly rising toward the sun
No one knows what God has seen
As humankind destroyed this Garden
With bleeding hands we'll plant the seeds
And He'll make all things new again
God will make all things live again

Liezl's words stirred something in my heart about what the Lord was planning with this miracle child of ours.

The next afternoon, the boys and I found the nearest Woolworths using Google Maps. We were on a mission: Mission Blue Baby Clothes. Stéfan and Morné, too, needed a change of mindset, since they'd been convinced they would get a new sister (largely due to the fantasy of another baby girl that Franché and I had harboured). We bought booties, clothes, blankets and even washcloths—everything in blue.

The three of us took the first steps to show we chose to believe that God knew exactly what He was doing and that He was planning only good things for us. Just like He promises us in Jeremiah 29:11, another anchor verse for me.

The evening after the blue shopping trip in Stellenbosch, I met a friend from my university days for dinner at an Italian restaurant on a wine farm. We had a good laugh about the old days, told each other what had happened to us in the intervening years, during which we had only had contact on Facebook and spoken on the phone on birthdays. There were tears of joy, but also tears of sorrow.

At one point in the evening my friend had to go to the bathroom. I was looking around the restaurant when I noticed a curly-haired boy at the table opposite ours. From behind he looked a little like Mia, with longish blond locks. In that moment, the fidgety little boy managed to instil a firm conviction in my mind: It would be a boy and he would be a great blessing in our lives, more than we could ever have dreamt of or expected. It would far, far surpass the human dreams and the expectations that I'd dished up for myself.

I know that Mia could never ever be replaced, and I did not want this child ever to feel like a substitute. After all, the desire for another child had been there long before Mia "went home". It was just that a big hole had opened up next to this desire, which had only made it stronger. We'd coloured that desire pink instead of waiting to see what the Father's choice of colour would be for this picture.

I believed this boy would have qualities that would remind us of our special little girl whom we had with us for such a short time, just as he would have similar mannerisms and personality traits as his two brothers. But he would be a brand-new entity and a huge gift from the Father, a little miracle just for us.

That's how Stellenbosch, a place that had been a beacon of pain and longing since 2013, became a beacon of hope.

Samuel

Back in Bloemfontein, the weeks flew by. The life growing inside me became more and more evident every day. The fact that we were going to have a baby became a reality—also for my husband and our two sons, who could put their hands on my stomach to feel the baby move.

During this time, my friend Youla asked me a number of times whether we'd decided on a name yet. Each time I replied that we were still thinking and wondering about it. I chose not to say anything about Liezl's message. Youla, however, didn't keep quiet about what she'd heard. Samuel, she said. That's what she'd heard.

Soon after this conversation, our women's cell group got together. We talked about the miracle of my pregnancy. There had been many evenings when these same women had prayed and cried and hoped with me for another baby. Youla told everyone of her experience about the name of this baby. Wide-eyed, my friend Marizanne said that she'd had the same experience during quiet time at home a week before. I then told them that what they'd heard was a confirmation of what Liezl had experienced.

I could declare anew: we truly hear God's voice during our quiet times with Him.

During this time, the lyrics of songs written and sung by Christian artists often confirmed great truths for me, like when I discovered the song "Unplanned" by Matthew West "by chance." It further confirmed the names Matthys Samuel for me, as well as the fact that he would be healthy:

I'm looking at a masterpiece
I'm staring at a work of art
I'm listening to a symphony

In every beat of your tiny heart
You used to be a choice to make
But now I think you've chosen me
'Cause I see ten fingers, ten toes
Two eyes and I know this is meant to be

Broken turns to beautiful
I see you right before my eyes
And every single breath you breathe
Is destiny love has brought to life
I thought it was my story's end
But now the future's all I see

On 28 May 2019, I was 22 weeks along in my pregnancy and had to go for a check-up. My gynaecologist noticed that the wall in the lower segment of my uterus was very thin at the scars of my previous three caesarean sections. This thin wall posed a great risk for the pregnancy. I was given fairly strict instruction to take it much easier.

At 26 weeks, an ultrasound showed that the situation had worsened. Bed rest was the instruction, together with the warning: there's a high risk that things could go wrong.

Youla and my other friends then hurriedly moved up my baby shower to a Saturday morning early in July. All activities such as this had to stop before I was 30 weeks along. At the baby shower I gave my testimony about our miracle, and I revealed the names of our son: Matthys Samuel Robberts. Matthys means "glory to God" or "gift from God", and Samuel, of course, means "asked of the Lord, and God heard". Hannah's story was my story after all.

That morning, among a group of my friends, Tannie Hanja gave me a hug and said to me, "I feel I have to tell you that every day he stays inside is grace from God." Her words were meaningful, even though I didn't fully understand them yet.

That evening I had so much pain that I could barely walk. Five days later, after another ultrasound, I was admitted to hospital. I felt a strange relief, but I wasn't afraid at all. I firmly believed that this miracle would be to the glory of our Father, to the end. Despite everything the doctor had said, I experienced a supernaturally calm feeling that everything would be fine, no matter when the baby arrived.

The hospital's maternity ward was not an easy place to get used to. Within days, the members of my cell group had covered the four clinical white walls of my windowless room with photos of all my children and my husband. Wherever I looked, I could see them.

Our first goal was to reach the 30-week mark.

And we made it!

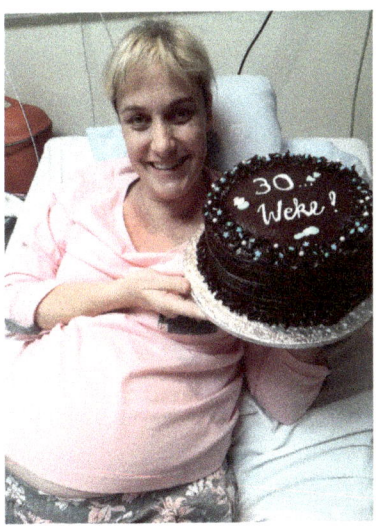

Charlene, my friend who bakes amazing cakes for a living, brought us a chocolate ganache cake so we as a family and the hospital staff could celebrate it together.

Daily messages and visits from numerous precious friends helped me to get through the sometimes-very-long days in the hospital room. I was even spoilt with a facial, manicure and pedicure one day—right there in my hospital bed!

I also made new friends in the hospital and sometimes went on outings to "their place": the tea room, about 10m from my room. There, the maternity ward sister and I drank tea and crocheted, like old ladies. I saw many women come and go. Like me, some had to stay longer "to keep their babies inside", whereas others just came to deliver them, often in the small hours of the night.

One of my forced pastimes was to listen to the labour sounds. Some women cried; others sounded like they were singing a lament; others screamed; and then there were those who, in between the contractions, fought with the father of their child. I had a good laugh a number of times about everything I heard.

The most precious sound of this concert was, of course, the first cry of every newborn. They sound like baby kittens that suddenly start to meow. It's the most beautiful sound—the sound of new life.

Weekends in the hospital were difficult. It started to get quiet on a Friday afternoon once all the operating theatre cases had been dealt with. My visitors were also fewer over weekends, because my friends spent time with their families (as it should be), and my family couldn't stay with me the whole time. During these quiet times I had to remind myself to focus on why I was there and on what my reward would be.

The 32-week mark was on 7 August 2019; I'd been in the hospital for four weeks. Charlene was there again with sweet treats.

On this day of another milestone to celebrate in the clinical room, with a limited number of television channels available, only so many menu options (repeated, by the way, every few days), just so many crochet patterns and balls of wool, and only so many sets of pyjamas to rotate, I received an email.

The news was like a drop of fresh spring water: we'd received the first preliminary "yes" from a publisher to whom we'd submitted the manuscript of this book. A completely different milestone had been achieved, one that I'd worked on for a very long time, that had brought many tears, and that had confronted me anew with the pain of losing Mia.

Was it the beginning of something that would portray hope in a different way?

The weekend of 9 to 11 August was a particularly quiet and difficult one for me in that room. I again got the familiar feeling of my throat constricting, a feeling that I'd got to know very well in the years after the accident. It's a mixture of expecting something really special that you know will remain so, forever, and a sense of reality that cuts through you like a hot knife through butter.

During the previous week I'd told Monique, one of the nurses, about this feeling and the pain that I experienced every year in August.

Monday, 12 August 2019, would have been Mia's 10th birthday. That morning at 8 o'clock, when I heard the familiar high-heeled footsteps of my doctor in the corridor, it wasn't only for her daily drop-in and how-are-you-feeling visit. Together with the nurses, she'd brought me pink balloons, a pink birthday cake, a framed photo of Mia and a crocheted angel (sister Monique's handiwork).

It was a full day, full of contradictions, just like the journey after Mia's death. From early in the morning there were visitors who brought flowers and sweets. There was also another email, this time a second yes to Mia's book, "by chance" on this special day on our family's calendar.

At the end of that busy, special day in my cave, as I'd dubbed the hospital room, I could turn off the light and just thank my Heavenly Father for it. The cave was not so dark.

After 12 August, the wheelchair lunches over weekends with my family also came to an end. The tea-room visits with the sisters ceased being the highlight of my day because sitting and walking had become too painful for me.

On Wednesday, 14 August—at 33 weeks—I received an encouraging message from Liezl. Among others, she wrote about a dream she'd had: "I dreamt that Samuel had been born, and he weighed 2,64 kg and was 100% perfect."

That Friday, my doctor did an ultrasound and determined that Samuel weighed 2,363 kg. I told her about Liezl's dream and she said she would be happy with that weight.

And that's how week five in the cave ended.

On Wednesday, 21 August, we reached the 34-week milestone. We had cake again. How many more cakes would Charlene bring? The ultrasound of that week gave an estimated weight of 2,543 kg.

On Sunday, 25 August 2019, my gynaecologist decided that the contractions were getting too regular and too strong. I was added to the operating theatre list for the coming Wednesday. There was more than enough time to inject me again in case she wasn't happy with his lung development and to take me off my blood-thinning medication. I was greatly relieved that the daily injections I'd been getting for seven weeks would end. My swollen stomach was full of blue dots that looked like freckles as a result of the seven times seven needle pricks.

On Tuesday, 27 August, one day before Matthys would be born, I received the message that Mia's book would definitely be published.

Divine coincidence? I preferred to call it divine planning. This perfect divine timing runs like a golden thread through Mia's story, our story, my story. And when you really think about it, also through your story.

Tannie Hanja's word at the beginning of 2017 took shape in the middle of 2019: "The Lord is waiting for you to write the book; only then will you fall pregnant." She'd never said that the book would be approved for publication the day before his birth.

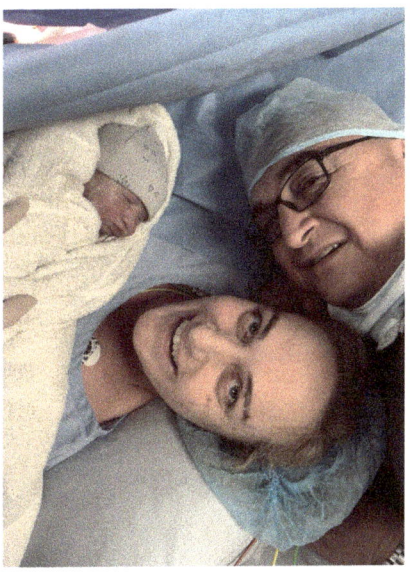

The miracle happened at 08:33 on Wednesday, 28 August 2019. I was exactly 35 weeks pregnant. In the operating theatre there was unprecedented excitement about Matthys Samuel's weight. Diana, the sister who was with us in the theatre and had been with me on this seven-week-long journey, came to me with him in her arms and said: "When I put him down on the scale, it showed 2,64 kg, and then it rolled back to 2,63 kg."

The feeling of gratitude was overwhelming for both Franché and me. God is so faithful. No matter how long it takes, we felt, His Word stands forever.

Stéfan and Morné had waited outside the theatre. When Matthys was wheeled out, my husband could take the most beautiful photograph of the two proud brothers with their new brother. The junction of the difficult path they'd walked after the loss of their little sister and the pride in their new little brother is one of the most cherished moments in my mother's-heart. The photo of them standing next to the incubator, chests swelled with pride, will be a permanent one in the library of pictures in my head.

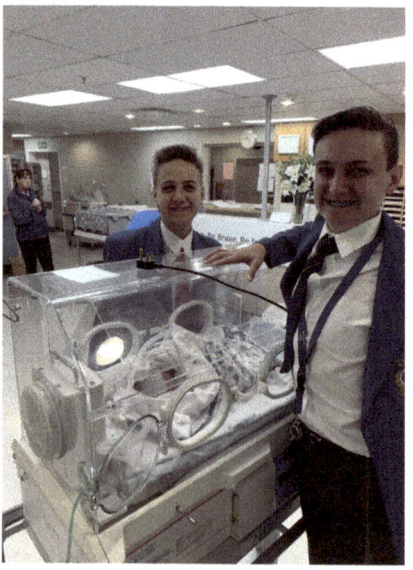

Matthys was taken straight to the newborn nursery, but later that day they put him on oxygen, just to help him a little since he had to work very hard for every breath he took. Later in the afternoon they took him to the neonatal unit so they could keep a close eye on him. They helped to increase his lung capacity a bit and ventilated him. As a precaution, they also gave him antibiotics.

The next morning the paediatrician began to wean him off the oxygen. He had no problem breathing ambient air. A day later I could hold him against my body. Two days later I was discharged, and another two days later we could take Matthys home.

Our son was born four weeks early, but I was granted my wish that he wouldn't have to remain in the neonatal unit for weeks on end.

It was spring by the time we were all back at home. I had spent the winter in hospital and had missed 53 days of bare trees and bitterly cold winds. As I was sitting inside my house, writing the final words for Mia's book, the Robberts family's book, I could smell the jasmine flowers in our garden. Matthys's birth was now a part of the story. At one stage I looked up from the computer screen at the dressing table where a vase of pink tulips had stood a few years before. This time, the vase contained purple tulips that my friend Anna had brought us.

They were still tulips, but now they reflected purple, for us a symbol of the fulfilment of another chapter of hope in our lives. Hope for every member of the Robberts family, each of whom at one time or another have had to face the world with desperation in the eyes. Franché and I know in our hearts that not only Matthys Samuel but also Stéfan and Morné have a great purpose here on earth.

Each of them has a life with a voice, as Matthew West sings:

Every life deserves a voice
Every child deserves a chance
You are more than just a choice
There's no such thing as unplanned

Psalm 139:16 (The Passion Translation) sums it up in one sentence:

You saw who you created me to be before I became me.

Thank You, Heavenly Father.
Hope comes to the fore in our lives in so many shades.

I wanna build you a garden
In a dry and desert land

Indeed, Jason Upton, indeed. A garden has been planted.

Conclusion

Not reaching back for what was lost in my yesterdays. And not reaching for what I hope will be in my tomorrow. But living fully with what is right in front of me. And truly seeing the gift of this moment.
– Lysa TerKeurst, *Becoming More Than a Good Bible Study Girl*

In her book *Becoming More Than a Good Bible Study Girl*, Lysa TerKeurst writes that everything in the process of dealing with loss and grief takes time.

It takes time, even when you love God and believe in His promises. Even when you believe you will see your loved one again, it takes time before that knowledge can begin to console you.

You sometimes stumble aimlessly, hopelessly lost, wading through an ocean of tears.

It takes searching for and finding a possession of your loved one that you thought was lost and realising God did that to comfort you. It takes being surprised to find yourself smiling for the first time after all the hurt.

It takes prayer. And there comes a day when you're compelled to make the decision to stop asking for answers and start asking for perspective.

It takes telling people not to avoid saying her name in your presence. It takes time to be able to say: I want to hear it, over and over and over again. Say "Mia", because I've taken off the heavy blanket of grief and put it away.

It's still here in my cupboard, folded up. On cold evenings I take it out, because in the folds of that blanket lie the wonderful experiences I have tried to convey on the pages of this book.

It takes time, the great Potter reassures us.

When a Father Mourns

The moment that the Vito collided with the tractor wheel, time slowed down. It was absolutely quiet. I felt the vehicle flying through the air for what seemed like a long time. The next moment there was a thud, and then it rolled twice, perhaps three times. I remember trying to protect my head with my hands as we were rolling and rolling and rolling.

Once we'd come to a standstill, I saw Mariska next to me and my mind registered that she was okay. I heard Stéfan, Morné and Pauline screaming. I didn't hear Mia. My door wouldn't open and I crawled out of the window. That's when I saw Mia lying on the ground about 15 m away. I ran to her to pick her up, but as I started to lift her I noticed that her neck was limp so I laid her down. I thought she might be unconscious and I didn't want to cause her further injury by picking her up.

I ran around the Vito to where Mariska was standing with Pauline and Stéfan and Morné, who were sitting and lying on the grass; the three of them were crying.

I ran back to where Mia was still lying in the same position on the ground; again, I wanted to pick her up. I touched the back of her head, and I felt and saw something viscous. Mariska and I both later realised that it had probably been some of her brain tissue.

I returned to Mariska, knowing she would ask me whether Mia was okay. Never in my life will I forget Mariska's expression when she asked me where Mia was, and I answered: "I think Miemie is gone."

Mariska ran to where Mia was lying on the grass. I remember the sound of her scream as if it happened yesterday.

In the next half-hour or so a number of people pulled off the road. Some offered to call an ambulance. One man felt Mia's pulse, and I could hear him saying to someone, "The ambulance had better get here quickly." Meanwhile, my two sons cried and cried, and Mariska and I both knew our little girl was gone.

In the ambulance, as the five of us, without Mia, were driven away from the accident scene, the boys cried and screamed that we couldn't leave Mia behind. I called my mother from the ambulance and simply told her we'd been in an accident and that Mia was gone. She started to sob.

A friend from Bloemfontein, Heinrich, met us at the hospital, as did our friend Thea, whom we'd planned to meet for lunch later.

I remember other faces from that day: my sister, Ilzette; and our pastor from Bloemfontein, Neville, who, when he heard the news, immediately got on a plane to come and support us. I remember forcing down some KFC just to get food in my stomach.

On that dark day I couldn't know yet what a major role Neville would play in my life. I used to be religious, but he helped me to become a real child of God.

A couple of days later, our disconsolate family flew back to Bloemfontein with Mia's ashes. The 10 days between the accident and the memorial service was a time of overwhelming fatigue, even though I didn't go to work. Mariska was shattered, and the boys were at home because the third school term hadn't started yet. Our house was filled with people, flowers, trays of food, and numerous religious booklets, which brought no consolation at all.

I remember fragments from that time, like people hugging us and commiserating with us, a pink memorial service that resembled a kids' party, and me being completely devastated.

I returned to work and the children returned to school soon after Mia's memorial service, but Mariska didn't get out of bed. She slept, prayed, wrote and cried. Every day, all day long. The only break in this routine was when she fetched the boys from school. There were times when we wept together, but there were also times when I argued with her and begged her to get up. I knew I couldn't reproach her, but I so badly wanted her to get on with life.

One morning she told me of her vision of Mia with Jesus and our late friend Mari. I wondered by myself whether she was delusional, but then I also remembered the tears and goosebumps after she'd told me about Liezl, a then-stranger who'd given her pink tulips completely unexpectedly. The signs of God's omnipresence in our lives were difficult to ignore. My first true spiritual journey started the day Mariska told me about Liezl's tulips. I wanted what she had, and still has.

To this day I often wonder what Mia would have looked like at this age. I wonder, would she have liked boys yet? I still cry over her, but we don't cry about the accident anymore.

At Mia's memorial service we declared that we'd chosen to trust God's plan for our lives. On that day we didn't fully grasp the impact of our words. Today, I know there's no other way we could have made it.

Franché Robberts

A Letter to Parents Who've Lost a Child

Dear Mom and Dad

You have to realise that one of the worst, most difficult, most painful, most incomprehensible and most inexplicable things in life has happened to you.

There are no quick fixes, techniques or guidelines that will help to take your pain away. It's a process that you have to go through, the process of grieving. It has started, and you have to go through it and learn to survive. The grieving process is intensely difficult and there is no set timetable. The pain is unspeakable.

Yet it is a process during which and through which one can grow. Often, this growth is as slow as the hour-hand of a clock. You cannot see it move while you're staring at it, but after a while you will see that there has been movement. You'll only recognise this growth in hindsight.

God carries you through this grieving process. He carries you not only on the days when you're aware of it, but also on those days when you feel like God has deserted you. Hold fast to His many promises, especially the one in Romans 8:31–39.

There is an old proverb, "Time heals all wounds." This is not true. Time in itself does not heal the raw wounds of loss. The crucial part is what you *do* during the process of grieving to deal with your loss.

Be mindful of and prepared for the following:

What people say

People will, with the best of intentions, say the most absurd things in an effort to comfort you. Their words will likely stun, bewilder, frustrate and even anger you. Some of the typical things people say to grieving parents are that "God picked his most beautiful flower," "God needed her," or "Everything that happens is God's will."

These statements are simply not true. Nor is the caricature of God that they create.

These people's motives might be sincere, but their words reflect clumsiness and ignorance.

They have no idea how you feel.

Changes in you

After the death of a child, parents experience a complete shift in priorities. Suddenly, things that you used to consider important parts of your daily routine hold little to no interest for you anymore. You are actually amazed at how worked-up people can get about minor issues.

Mercifully, the opposite is also true. Things that used to seem insignificant and that you often took for granted get new meaning and could play an important role in the grieving process. Something like the pink shade of a sunset.

You will probably find that you're no longer in step with the world and with your friends.

Men and women grieve differently

The following guidelines are, of course, generalisations, but they might be of value to you.

Men tend to grieve much more rationally, whereas women grieve more "emotionally". For men, it's important to know the facts and the details of events; it helps them to process their loss. Women, on the other hand, attach greater value to emotional experiences. A man would try his best to be strong for the sake of his wife, in the hope, of course, that it would alleviate her suffering. Unfortunately, this sometimes has a negative impact on the relationship. The wife could get the wrong impression that her husband's grief is not as intense as hers. It could even lead to the misperception that she is overreacting.

Talk to each other, even though you're both hurting so much that it's difficult to do so. My advice for a husband is to communicate to his wife that he is experiencing grief and that he is having a hard time, even though he is trying not to show it.

Because men and women are so fundamentally different in how they grieve and mourn, it's essential that they're patient with each other, that they give each other space, and that they're aware of the normal but diverse ways of dealing with death.

Loyalty is an integral part of a woman's, and especially a mother's, grieving process. Mothers are the most loyal beings in creation. For a mother it is of the utmost importance that she *never* forgets her child and, crucially, that her memories of her child won't fade. This often results in her not allowing herself enjoyment. Feelings of guilt tend to develop if she enjoys something while this unspeakable pain rages inside her. Being aware that loyalty plays an important role in the grieving process can be of great value. It can help a husband and wife better understand each other's actions and reactions.

After the death of a child, a parent's relationship with God usually goes through several distinct stages. These stages are different for everyone; you cannot predict what they will look like. They could differ radically from one person to the next.

Some people go through a phase of interrogating God. "Why, Lord?" "Why our child?" "Why now?" "Why did she have to die like this?" "Why?"

It's common for parents—both believers and unbelievers—to be angry at God and to blame Him for the death of the child; it is a normal reaction. Do not condemn it. See it as sincere wrestling with God and a genuine search for answers to questions that could never really be answered satisfactorily.

Mercifully, most believers will find that their relationship with God intensifies and deepens amid their tragedy and struggle. Just be aware that, often, this does not happen quickly and easily; it is a process of gradual growth.

A biblical event that illustrates this practically is God's provision of manna to His children during the wilderness period after the exodus from Egypt. God provided manna, but only enough for one day's survival. It was a daily reminder for them to put their trust in God, and every day they could experience His wonderful, gracious provision anew. So great is God's grace that He provided a double portion on the sixth day of every week so that they didn't have to work on the Sabbath.

During the grieving process one comes to know that God is always faithful, but that He does not provide everything at once or makes the sadness disappear like mist before the sun.

Your other children

Many people who have lost a sibling through early death would tell you that they subsequently lost their parents through grief.

The death of a child is so overwhelming and all-consuming that a parent often doesn't have the emotional or physical strength to pay proper attention to the needs of their surviving children. It is a normal reaction and it's understandable, but children can suffer great emotional damage as a result.

It is normal for every conversation to end up being about the child who died. It is normal for parents to have photos of the child who died enlarged and to display them prominently. But at some point, somehow, you have to turn your focus to your other children. Despite your unbearable pain, you have to be there for their activities, get excited about their achievements, and sometimes just talk to them about *them* and not about the brother or sister who died.

May every parent who reads this book and thus shares in the Robberts family's sad journey get a new perspective. May you also be touched and comforted by God through their sincere struggle. And may this book about spiritual growth in God touch the lives and hearts of many people.

Braam Klopper
Minister and pastoral therapist

Dedication

I dedicate this book to a very special little girl, my Mia Muis; I am so grateful that you were a part of our lives, and still are, and always will be: Mia Ananja Robberts, 12 August 2009—27 March 2013.

A special thank you to my husband, Franché, and my children, Stéfan, Morné and Matthys. And to Pauline. You were and are fellow travellers on this painful journey to healing.

Thank you very much to every family member and friend for your prayers and the numerous ways in which you showed us that you care. Friends are God's way of taking care of us.

Liezl, thank you for your obedience to our Father. You painted a bright pink streak of hope in my life—more than once. Without you there might not even have been a book. Thank you, Erika—you kept pestering me to start writing; and Tannie Hanja, for serving God with a loyal heart.

Colette, my friend, how can I ever thank you enough for your compassion and for the hours and hours of weaving together this story. We did it!

Maretha Maartens, thank you for your wisdom and your guidance through the writing process.

Above all, thank you to my Father in heaven. Thank you for my very special family. Thank you for every friend that You've brought into my life; they have been extensions of Your hands. Thank you for Mia. Thank you for your presence and solace through the years. Thank you for every encounter with Mia to console me. Thank you for really being a Father on this journey and for placing instances of hope in my path for me to find. Our family look to You and place our hope in You to provide for us on our life journey. All glory to You. Amen.

Bibliography

Bereavement: Reactions, Consequences, and Care by the National Academy of Sciences, 1984

Didion, Joan. *The Year of Magical Thinking*. Knopf Doubleday, 2005

The Everyday Life Bible: Amplified Version, featuring notes and commentary by Joyce Meyer. Warner Faith, 2006

Lewis, C.S. *A Grief Observed*. Faber & Faber, 1961

McPherson, Retha and Aldo. *A Message from God*, Corals, 2007

TerKeurst, Lysa. *Becoming More Than a Good Bible Study Girl*. Zondervan, 2012

Upton, Jason. "The Garden Song" from the album *Glimpse*, 2012

Upton, Jason. "Samuel" from the album *Dying Star*, 2002

West, Matthew. "Unplanned" from the album *Unplanned*, 2019

Readers...

Thank you for reading *Mia*.
If you have a moment, please review *Mia* at the store where you bought it.

Help other readers by telling them why you would recommend this book. No need to write an in-depth discussion. Even a single sentence will be greatly appreciated. Reviews go a long way to helping a book sell, and is great to help spread the word. It'll also help us to continue publishing quality books.

Thank you again for taking the time to journey with Crystal Lake Publishing.